THOMAS COOK
Travellers

KT-379-695

MALLORCA

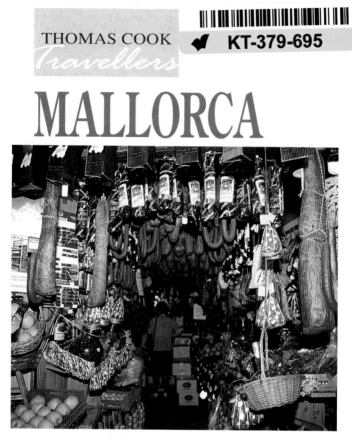

BY
NIGEL TISDALL

Produced by AA Publishing

Written by Nigel Tisdall

Original photography by Peter Baker

Edited, designed and produced by AA Publishing.
© The Automobile Association 1995.
Maps © The Automobile Association 1995.
Reprinted 1995

A CIP catalogue record for this book is available from the
British Library.

ISBN 0 7495 0960 0

The contents of this publication are believed correct at the time of
printing. Nevertheless, the publishers cannot accept responsibility for
any errors or omissions, or for changes in the details given in this guide
or for the consequences of any reliance on the information provided by
the same. Assessments of attractions, hotels, restaurants and so forth are
based upon the author's own experience and therefore descriptions
given in this guide necessarily contain an element of subjective opinion
which may not reflect the publisher's opinion or dictate a reader's own
experiences on another occasion.
**We have tried to ensure accuracy in this guide, but things do
change and we would be grateful if readers would advise us of
any inaccuracies they may encounter.**

Published by AA Publishing (a trading name of Automobile Association
Developments Limited, whose registered office is Norfolk House,
Priestley Road, Basingstoke, Hampshire RG24 9NY. Registered number
1878835) and the Thomas Cook Group Ltd.

Colour separation: BTB Colour Reproduction, Whitchurch,
Hampshire.

Printed by Edicoes ASA, Oporto, Portugal.

Cover picture: *Cala Sant Vicenç*
Title page: *shopping in Palma*
Above: *fresh orange juice awaits in Valldemossa*

Contents

About this Book

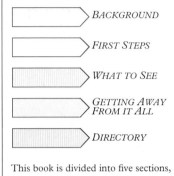

BACKGROUND

FIRST STEPS

WHAT TO SEE

GETTING AWAY
FROM IT ALL

DIRECTORY

This book is divided into five sections,
identified by the above colour coding.

Background gives an introduction to
the island – its history, geography,
politics, culture.

First Steps offers practical advice on
arriving and getting around.

What to See is an alphabetical listing of
places to visit, interspersed with walks
and tours.

Getting Away From it All highlights
places off the beaten track where it's
possible to relax and enjoy peace and
quiet.

Finally, the **Directory** provides practical
information – from shopping and
entertainment to children and sport,
including a section on business matters.
Special highly illustrated features on
specific aspects of the island appear
throughout the book.

Peace and quiet in Cala Figuera, a pretty
fishing cove in the south of the island

BACKGROUND

'Here I am in the midst of palms and cedars and cactuses and olives and lemons and aloes and figs and pomegranates. The sky is turquoise blue, the sea is azure, the mountains are emerald green; the air is as pure as that of Paradise.'

FREDERIC CHOPIN
1838

Introduction

*M*allorca might have been invented by a team of tourism gurus locked in a *tapas* bar with a brief to come up with a holiday island that could please as many people as possible.

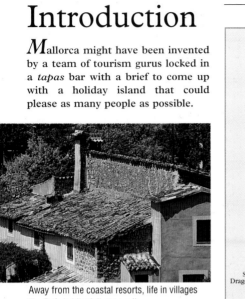

Away from the coastal resorts, life in villages like Deía is blissfully tranquil

As a well-established Mediterranean resort it has everything you would expect: good sandy beaches, guaranteed summer sunshine, safe water for swimming, hotel and self-catering accommodation to suit all pockets. If you like pretty mountain villages and photogenic harbours, family amusements and watersports, golf courses and excursions in glass-bottomed boats, intimate fish restaurants where the sun sets on a sea of luxury yachts – it's all here.

But there is more, a Mallorca that scarcely needs the cooing of the brochures. Palma, the capital, has a dramatic seafront cathedral and old streets with an authentic whiff of history. There are enthralling underground caves and isolated hilltop monasteries to seek out, epic mountains much loved by walkers and cyclists, and marshes and offshore islands that regularly draw birdwatchers.

MALLORCA

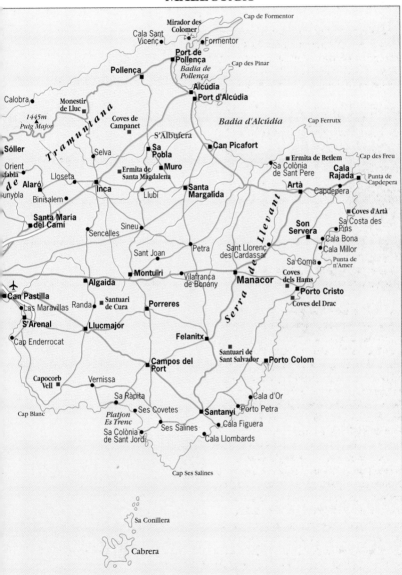

Cap de Formentor

Mirador des Colomer

Cala Sant Vicenç

Formentor

Port de Pollença

Pollença

Badia de Pollença

Cap des Pinar

Alcúdia

Port d'Alcúdia

Calobra

Monestir de Lluc

1445m
Puig Major

Coves de Campanet

S'Albufera

Badia d'Alcúdia

Cap Ferrutx

Sóller

Selva

Sa Pobla

Can Picafort

Ermita de Betlem

Cap des Freu

Orient
Bàfabia

Alaró

Lloseta

Ermita de Santa Magdalena

Muro

Sa Colònia de Sant Pere

Cala Rajada

Punta de Capdepera

unybla

Binisalem

Inca

Llubí

Santa Margalida

Artà

Capdepera

Coves d'Artà

Santa María del Camí

Sencelles

Sineu

Sa Costa des Pins

Son Servera

Cala Bona

Cala Millor

Petra

Sant Llorenç des Cardassar

Sant Joan

Sa Coma

Punta de n'Amer

Montuïri

Vilafranca de Bonány

Manacor

Coves dels Hams

Algaida

Porto Cristo

Can Pastilla

Las Maravillas

Randa

Santuari de Cura

Porreres

Coves del Drac

S'Arenal

Llucmajor

Felanitx

Cap Enderrocat

Santuari de Sant Salvador

Porto Colom

Campos del Port

Capocorb Vell

Vernissa

Sa Ràpita

Cala d'Or

Platjon Es Trenc

Ses Covetes

Santanyí

Porto Petra

Cap Blanc

Ses Salines

Cála Figuera

Sa Colònia de Sant Jordi

Cala Llombards

Cap Ses Salines

Sa Conillera

Cabrera

Tramuntana

de Alaró

Serra de Llevant

Geography

*T*he Balearic Islands lie 82km east of the Spanish mainland in the Mediterranean Sea. Mallorca is the largest island, roughly 100km from east to west. Menorca, only a fifth of Mallorca's size, lies 40km to its east while the even smaller island of Ibiza, also known as Eivissa, is 85km to the southwest. Formentera, hanging close to Ibiza's southern coast, completes an archipelago attended by another hundred tiny islands.

BALEARIC ISLANDS

d'Alcúdia in the northeast and Badia de Palma in the west, now home to the island's capital, Palma. The small uninhabited island of Sa Dragonera lies just off the island's western tip, and 18km south of Mallorca is Cabrera, the largest in a cluster of tiny islands that are now a nature park.

Geology

The mountains of Mallorca are part of the Baetic Cordillera, a range of peaks that runs southwest through Ibiza to southern Andalucía and Cádiz. The island is predominantly limestone and in

Landscape

A range of domineering mountains, the Serra de Tramuntana, runs the length of Mallorca's northwest coast. The highest peaks gather in the centre around the island's summit, Puig Major (1,445m). A second lower mountain range, the Serra de Llevant, runs like an echo across the southeast of the island. Its highest point, Puig de Sant Salvador, rises to 510m and is capped by a famous religious sanctuary. Between these mountains lies Es Pla, a flat cultivated plain dotted with windmills and small agricultural towns.

Mallorca's coastline stretches for some 555km. In the north high cliffs fall abruptly to the sea, while the east coast is indented with *calas* (coves). Two great sandy bays gnaw into the island, Badia

places severe erosion has created deep canyons and extraordinary caves that have become major tourist attractions. The rich soil in the central plain gets its striking reddish-brown colour from iron oxide deposits.

Climate

Mallorca enjoys a Mediterranean climate with mild winters and hot, dry summers. The mountains of the Serra de Tramuntana attract the greatest rainfall, and are sometimes capped with snow in winter. They act as a buffer against winds from the north, while sea breezes temper the heat of the summer months.

Population

The population of Mallorca is 613,000, of whom 325,000 live in Palma. In addition, every year 5 million tourists visit the island, attracting an influx of seasonal staff to serve them. An idea of the lop-sided effect tourism has on the island's character can be gauged from the fact that the resort of Cales de Mallorca has a resident population of only 250, yet accommodation for 8,500 visitors.

Steep-sloping, pine-forested cliffs run the length of Mallorca's northwest coast

Economy

A favourite topic of conversation among Mallorcans is the death of the island's agriculture. As a result of the tourist boom, two-thirds of the island's working population are now employed in the service sector. That fruit growing so picturesquely in fields, orchards and olive groves is often never picked, and staircases of abandoned terraces are a frequent and poignant sight in the

Vegetables, salad crops and fruit are cultivated in the fertile soil around Sa Pobla

remoter parts of the island. Agriculture is still commercially viable on the central plain, helped by modern methods and irrigation, and grants are given to landowners to keep their property in shape – which usually means employing sheep as lawnmowers. In urban areas, the construction industry and factories manufacturing shoes, garments and costume jewellery provide sources of employment, but tourism is the overwhelming mainstay of the island's economy.

TALAIOTIC CULTURE

The Balearic Islands were originally settled by an industrious and well-organised people who left enigmatic visiting cards around Mallorca known as *talaiots*. These megalithic monuments get their name from *atalaya,* the Arab word for watchtower, and have become eponymous symbols of the talented civilisation that flourished here during the Bronze Age.

The Talaiot Period came in three waves. Pre-Talaiotic culture started around 2000BC and was principally cave-based. By 1500BC *navetes,* burial chambers that resemble upturned boats, were being constructed – there are abundant examples on Menorca. The most creative phase, the Talaiotic, lasted from 1300BC until about 800BC and coincided with the emergence of

a more violent and hierarchical society. A third stage, Late Talaiotic, is characterised by the construction of *taulas*, colossal table-like stone structures which are well preserved in Menorca. By the 6th century BC, Talaiotic culture was on the wane as the islands came under the influence of the Greeks and Phoenicians.

Archaeological research and evidence from similar cultures in

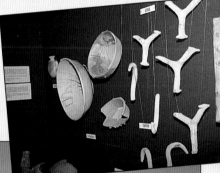

The ruins at Capocorb Vell; displays in the Museu de Mallorca, Palma

Sardinia and Corsica suggest that life in Talaiotic times was surprisingly sophisticated. The islanders kept sheep, pigs and cattle, constructed ingenious wells and made a delicate, decorated pottery.

Talaiots were built to both circular and quadrangular plans, and were most likely constructed as main residences and observation posts in the islands' fortified settlements. On Mallorca the best opportunities to inspect them are at Capocorb Vell and Ses Païsses. Archaeological finds from the period, including ceramics, weapons, tools and jewellery, can be seen in the Museu de Mallorca in Palma and the Museu Regional in Artà.

History

5000BC
Remains found in caves near Sóller and Valldemossa indicate the presence of humans on the island.

1300–800BC
Talaiotic culture flourishes in Mallorca and Menorca, leaving enigmatic stone towers and ruined dwellings at sites like Capocorb Vell and Ses Païsses.

1000–123BC
Phoenician, Greek and Carthaginian traders visit the Balearics. The islands' collective name probably derives from the Greek verb *ballein*, meaning 'to throw' – a reference to the leather slings used as deadly weapons by the islanders.

123BC–AD425
The Roman commander Quintus Cecilius Metullus conquers Mallorca. The island is called Balearis Major (hence its modern name) and a capital is established at Pollentia, now Alcúdia, where a Roman theatre survives.

❖

THOMAS COOK'S MALLORCA
Cook's first advertised Mallorca as part of a conducted tour to the Balearics in the winter of 1903. Potential visitors were informed that 'the climate of Palma rivals that of Málaga and Algiers' and that they could visit the Cathedral, La Llotja (Lonja), bullring, casino and quaint 16th-century houses. In 1905 the island was promoted as one of the best places to view the eclipse of the sun, due to take place on 30 August that year. It was popular as a 'Winter Paradise' destination before the advent of the package holiday.

❖

Christianity takes hold during the 2nd century AD.

425–707
With the decline of the Roman Empire, Mallorca comes under Vandal and Byzantine rule.

707–1229
Raids by the Moors accompany their conquest of mainland Iberia – by 902 Mallorca is part of the Emirate of Córdoba. The Moors build mosques, palaces and gardens and introduce sophisticated agricultural methods using windmills and waterwheels. In Palma, then known as Medina Mayurqa, the Banys Àrabs (Arab Baths) are a sign of their presence.

1229–1492
During the *Reconquista*, the reconquest of Spain by the Christians, Jaume I of Aragón lands at Santa Ponça and takes the island. Under his son, Jaume II, Mallorca enjoys a Golden Age that produces the Castell de Bellver and the polymath Ramón Llull. Mallorca's brief spell as an independent kingdom ends in 1349 with the defeat of Jaume III at Llucmajor. By 1492, following the union of Castile and Aragón and the defeat of the Moors at Granada, the island is a part of Spain.

16th to 18th centuries
The island's fortunes decline as Spain turns its attention to the New World. Watchtowers and fortified churches are built in response to repeated attacks from pirates. Mallorca backs the losing side in the War of the Spanish Succession (1701–14), and receives an influx of refugees after the French Revolution.

19th to early 20th century
During the Napoleonic Wars (1803–15)

thousands of French prisoners are abandoned on the island of Cabrera. Frédéric Chopin and George Sand stay in the monastery at Valldemossa during the winter of 1838–9, three years after the abolition of religious orders in Spain. A regular steamship service links Mallorca to the mainland, and in 1875 the islands' first railway line opens. Archduke Luis Salvador of Austria, a dedicated advocate of Mallorca's virtues, settles on the island.

1936–9
Spanish Civil War. Quickly seized by the Nationalists, Mallorca becomes a base for assaults on the mainland with the help of Italian forces. Menorca supports the Republicans.

1939–75
Dictatorship of General Franco. By the early 1960s Mallorca is at the forefront of Spain's tourist boom. After Franco's death, monarchy returns with King Juan Carlos I.

1983
The Balearic Islands become an autonomous region of Spain with Palma as its capital.

1986
Spain joins the European Community.

1992
The summer Olympics in Barcelona and Expo '92 in Seville trumpet the arrival of the new Spain. Five million tourists visit Mallorca.

Jaume I, the conqueror of Mallorca, now re-conquered by pigeons in Plaça d'Espanya

Culture

Mallorca's long-standing tag as the Isla de la Calma (Island of Calm) might seem absurd amid the disco frenzy of Magaluf or the lobster-bodied beaches of Cala Millor, but prior to the arrival of mass tourism the island was a bastion of tranquillity and tradition.

The Mallorcans

'Caution and reserve are the ruling trends of the Mallorcan character,' George Sand declared in her notorious travel book *A Winter in Majorca.* Mallorcans add a muted strand to the Spanish national character: they might not have the flamboyance of the Sevillians or the cosmopolitan buzz of citizens of Madrid or Barcelona, but they do possess the appealing virtues of politeness, placidity and prudence found in many other Mediterranean communities and small islands in general.

Discussing world problems in a café in Muro

Religion

The Catholic Church has held sway on Mallorca since the Reconquest. The Christians raised new churches on the site of Moorish mosques, and you will find chapels and sanctuaries built in the most obscure corners of the island. Since the death of Franco the influence of the church has declined, and few islanders under 40 regularly attend services. Nevertheless Mallorca remains a conformist society moulded by church, family and school. Every year some 50,000 islanders make a pilgrimage to the monastery at Lluc, home of Mallorca's patron saint, La Moreneta. Even a little-known sanctuary, like the Ermita de Sant Blai outside Campos del Port, will attract a saint's day procession of over 2,000 walkers and cyclists.

Life in the slow lane: in the country they still like to take things easy

Folklore

Mallorca's folklore reflects the insularity of its history. Look behind the sunshine and holiday euphoria of today, and the sky darkens with medieval fatalism and superstition. Delve into Mallorcan folk tales, and you find jocular explanations of why the poor are a necessary thing, or how women came to have less brains than men. The author Robert Graves claimed that witches were still practising on the island when he arrived in 1929. They are said to have favoured abandoned *talaiots* for their occult assemblies, and a favourite piece of Mallorcan witchcraft involved using a bull's horn anointed with olive oil to curse victims.

Island folklore as presented in hotels and dinner shows appears woefully sanitised in comparison, and tends to concentrate on coy courtship dances in colourful costume. Catch some of the island's religious celebrations though, like Semana Santa (Easter) with its processions of hooded penitents, or the more anarchic moments in the village *fiesta* when the firework-brandishing devils take over, and you get an inkling of the historic fears and impulses that underpin Mallorcan culture.

Small and intriguing art galleries, like this one in Deía, are found all over Mallorca

Education

Cultural life on Mallorca benefits from the presence of the island's Universitat des Illes Baleares, a university founded in 1978 which now has some 12,000 students. Spanish males between the ages of 18 and 27 have to do nine months' military service, and Mallorca is one of the most desirable postings in the country.

Art

Boosted by the profits from tourism, Mallorca has developed a reputation as an island that nurtures artists. Children are encouraged to attend art classes and exhibitions from an early age, and many wealthy islanders and visitors from the mainland have started collecting art. The population of Pollença is only 12,000, yet it has at least a dozen art galleries. Inspired by the famous light and landscape of Mallorca, encouraged by the aesthetic achievements of the late Joan Miró and the success of the young Felanitx-born painter Miquel Barceló, many young Mallorcans are getting involved with the arts. At the same time new exhibition spaces are being opened in Palma's historic buildings, and there is a revival of interest in the island's flamboyant Modernista (Spanish art nouveau) architecture.

PACKAGING PARADISE

Mallorca's phenomenal development as a tourist island is now the stuff of textbooks. The French even coined a derogatory verb, *baléariser*, to describe this evolution, and the Mallorcan model has been copied in coastal resorts from North Africa to the Caribbean. Today tourism is taught as a subject in the island's state-run university, and in Palma a private Escuela de Turismo (School of Tourism) draws hundreds of students from around the world to learn the art of running hotel chains, creating Paradise and packaging up holidaymakers for profit.

Though well-heeled tourists were discovering the island in the late 19th century, it was only after World War II that visitors began coming here in great numbers. In 1931 Mallorca welcomed 43,000 tourists; by 1950 there were 127,000. This sudden influx was chronicled with alarm by the island's resident sage, Robert Graves. 'Around 1951,' he wrote, 'British, French and American travellers accepted the fantasy of Majorca as the Isle of Love, the Isle of Tranquillity, the Paradise where the sun always shines and where one can live like a fighting cock on a dollar a day, drinks included.'

Once a refined winter sunshine resort, holidaymakers now flock to Mallorca for the beach, boat trips – and the breakfasts

Mallorca still draws an artistic crowd, though most impecunious Bohemians now prefer Ibiza. The drinks aren't so cheap either, and the well-documented days of the lager-fuelled *gamberros Ingleses* (English hooligans) and their Continental equivalents are just about over.

Today Mallorca is going upmarket and green – a time of new beaches and promenades, better hotels, ringroads and development controls to help loosen the collar of concrete shackling the coast. If these multi-million-peseta improvements do their stuff, the package holiday will be thriving here well into the next century, and the tourism students will have another chapter in the story of holiday Mallorca.

Politics

*T*he Balearic Islands have been an autonomous region of Spain since 1983. While language issues and the effects of tourism cause much debate, Mallorca is a stable and deeply conservative island.

Government

Spain is a constitutional monarchy, and the regular summer visits of King Juan Carlos I and the royal family to Mallorca bring pride and prestige to the island. As the largest and most influential island in the archipelago, Mallorca is the seat of the Govern Balear (Balearic Government). The regional parliament meets in the former Círculo Mallorquin building close to Palma cathedral. Out of a total of 59 seats, Mallorca has 33, Menorca 12, Ibiza 11 and Formentera 3. Political power has long rested with the conservative Partit Popular.

Flags outside the Balearic Parliament

THE HAZARDS OF CHANGE

One day Jesus and St Peter were out walking. They passed through a field of pumpkins, then a forest of oak trees.

'Wouldn't it be better,' St Peter asked, 'if pumpkins grew on oak trees, which have massive great trunks, and acorns grew on pumpkin plants, which have such flimsy stalks?'

'If you like,' replied Jesus.

At once there were pumpkins hanging from the trees, and bunches of acorns lying in the fields.

St Peter walked on, pleased with his improvement to the world. Suddenly a huge ripe pumpkin fell on his head, and knocked him to the ground.

'Is it such a good idea,' Jesus asked, 'to change what has been made?'

MALLORCAN FOLK TALE

Official language

As in Catalunya and Valencia on the mainland, the Catalan and Castilian languages have dual official status in the Balearic Islands. After decades of repression under Franco, the preservation and celebration of the Catalan language is seen by most islanders as the cornerstone of regional identity. Today Catalan predominates in the church, schools and university, but few Mallorcans are happy with the aggressive linguistic correctness of the radicals.

First Steps

'Simple, calm Majorca
is a green Switzerland
beneath a Calabrian sky,
and with the silent
solemnity of the Orient.'

George Sand
1842

First Steps

*M*allorca presents few problems to its visitors, though services and facilities can get strained at peak season. To get the best out of Mallorca, spend time picking the right resort and accommodation for your needs, then use this as a base for forays to other parts of the island.

When to go

Mallorca is very much a summer holiday resort, though great efforts are currently being made to make it attractive as a year-round destination. July and August are the peak months, with the season running between April and October. If you pay a visit outside of these times be prepared for poor weather. Many of the hotels close for at least part of the winter,

Another hard day's sightseeing in Port de Sóller, a resort favoured by French visitors

and the choice of excursions, restaurants and shops and the opening hours of sights are all considerably reduced. However, Palma never closes, and if lying on a sun-scorched beach is not your main objective, Mallorca can be very rewarding to visit in spring and late autumn when things are less hectic.

Where to stay

Most visitors to Mallorca stay in pre-booked accommodation – pick somewhere as close as possible to your preferred holiday option, be it on the seafront in Palma, rural isolation in a mountain farmhouse, or the round-the-clock partying of resorts like Palma Nova and S'Arenal. Bear in mind that most resorts, though superficially international, are often favoured by one or two nationalities in particular. For example, you will find the Germans gathering in S'Arenal, Scandinavians congregating in Cala Major, the French gravitating to Port de Sóller, and British contingents massing in Magaluf and Port de Pollença. Whether it is best to stay with or without your compatriots is another tough decision.

For the various types of accommodation available see pages 172–5.

Getting around

Wherever you stay on Mallorca, any other part of the island can be reached within a day trip. In recent years the

Try a tour of Palma by horse and carriage – Sunday is best, as there is less traffic

roads have greatly improved; if you are independent-minded, enjoy driving and like to get out into the peace of the mountains or visit the quieter beaches, it is well worth hiring a car for at least two or three days. While it is possible to zoom around the island in a day, it is better taken at a more leisurely pace. Four drives covering the best of Mallorca are included in this guide. They can each be done in around five hours, but it is preferable to make a day of it.

Public transport on the island is good. If you are staying outside Palma consider getting a bus into the capital rather than paying for a car you will hardly use. Buses get to most corners of the island, and the service is generally reliable. Tourist offices can supply you with a free timetable. Mallorca has two railway lines too, a historic line running from Palma through the Serra de Tramuntana to Sóller, and a half-hour run east to Inca.

The Mallorcan day

Organise your sightseeing around the fact that everything closes for lunch and a siesta between 1.30pm and 4.30pm. A notable exception is La Seu, Palma's cathedral, which stays open through the lunch hour in summer. Most smaller museums and art galleries close on Saturday afternoon and Sunday. In the evening you will find many restaurants have virtually two sittings: one for the tourists, and a second for the Spanish who like to eat late. The resorts live by their own laws: if there are people about and money to be made, the shops and bars stay open.

BEACHES AND COVES

One of the nicest jobs on Mallorca must be counting its beaches. The latest official tally was 74, of which 30 were awarded Blue Flags by the European Union for being safe, clean and well kept. Beaches are crucial to the success of tourism on the island, and the Mallorcans work hard to maintain standards in the resorts – most notably in the recent facelifts given to the seafronts in Palma Nova, Magaluf and S'Arenal.

If you come in summer, don't waste time trying to find that undiscovered, blissfully deserted beach. It is possible to get away from (most of) it all, but you will need to park your rented car and take a long, long walk. Until recently Platja Es Trenc in the south of the island fulfilled most people's isolationist dreams, but now even that has a car park and attendant at one end. There are no developments here though, and it is a popular spot for nude sunbathing and swimming. Nearer Palma, the tiny Platja Mago (off the road to Portals Vells) attracts a similar clothes-free crowd.

However, the majority of visitors

Packed and peaceful sands: Magaluf (left), Platja de Canyamel (above), Cala Llombards (right and below)

are happy to join the seething, sun-wallowing masses in the resorts. The most popular beaches are those around Badia de Palma, Badia d'Alcúdia and Badia de Pollença. On the east coast the tourist centres are Cala Bona, Cala d'Or, Cala Millor and Sa Coma.

Calas (coves) offer an enjoyable and quieter alternative to these well-

Beach promenade
at Can Pastilla

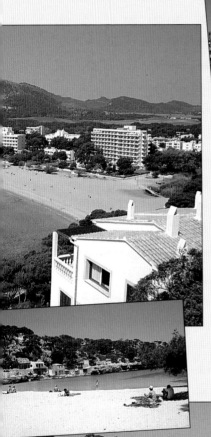

known hot-spots. High, deeply-eroded cliffs often shelter the sands at the end of these small inlets. The water tends to be invitingly clear – ideal for snorkelling, diving from the rocks, and for strong swimmers who feel frustrated by the shallow waters in the larger bays. Try Cala Pi (south of Llucmajor), Cala Llombards and Cala Santanyí (both east of Santanyí), or the larger beaches at Cala Agulla and Cala Mesquida (both north of Capdepera).

Finding the Sights

*T*he 'What to See' section of this guide (pages 28–132) divides Mallorca into five sections with sights arranged alphabetically in each. If your time is limited, you should try to spend a few hours in Palma and make a trip by car, train or bus into the mountains of the Serra de Tramuntana. The following highlights of the island are recommended.

PALMA

La Seu, Palma's seafront cathedral, is the island's star sight, but find time to visit La Llotja near by, once the city's maritime trading exchange. A walk along the seafront and Passeig des Born, the city's traditional promenade, is the statutory introduction to the Mallorcan capital, but don't miss the Fundació La Caixa, a splendidly-restored Modernista building in Plaça Weyler.

WEST OF PALMA

Well-developed resorts run all along the coast west of Palma. Get into the mountains behind them to visit the country house of La Granja and the tailor-made nature reserve, La Reserva. To see Mallorca in a different light, visit Porto Portals, an élite marina for the waterborne jet-set, and the Fundació Pilar i Joan Miró, the studio of the late surrealist painter Joan Miró.

NORTHWEST

This is the most accessible part of the Serra de Tramuntana. Take the Palma–Sóller train, and the tram ride on to Port de Sóller, for an insight into island life at the start of this century. The former Carthusian monastery at Valldemossa, where George Sand and Frédéric Chopin stayed during their visit of 1838–9, is an essential Mallorcan sight. The Moorish gardens at Alfabia, the spectacular descent down the northern cliffs to Sa Calobra, and the revered monastery at Lluc are all of interest.

NORTHEAST

Try to savour the time-worn atmosphere of at least a couple of Mallorca's ancient towns, such as Alcúdia, Artà, Petra or Pollença. Here the scenic draws are the

Steps lead up from the seafront to Palma's historic cathedral, La Seu, begun in 1230

Olive trees and a backdrop of mountains: a classic Mallorcan landscape near Andratx

Cap de Formentor peninsula, the illuminated subterranean caves at Artà, and the great sandy sweep of the Badia d'Alcúdia. Nature-lovers should make for the Bóquer valley and S'Albufera wetlands.

SOUTH

Crossing Es Pla, Mallorca's inland plain, is as crucial to understanding the island as touring its mountains. Drive up to the religious sanctuaries on Puig de Randa for an overview of this area, then relax in the quieter *calas* (coves) of the east coast.

There are large caves at Drac and Hams, prehistoric ruins at Capocorb Vell, and artificial pearl and glass factories along the Palma–Manacor road. If this all sounds too much, escape on a boat to the island of Cabrera.

SANTA CATALINA THOMAS
Pregau per nosaltres.

Sign language

Among the many entertaining sayings that bejewel life in this corner of Spain is '*No cridis el mal temps*', the Catalan equivalent of 'Don't yell for a bad time'. There is no need to learn Catalan before visiting Mallorca, but if you make the effort to learn even the smallest phrase you will be better received. Bear in mind, though, that local dialects survive in the mountain areas.

You have only to look at the island's vandalised road signs and street-names to see that language has become a contentious issue in Mallorca. Originally in Castilian, Spain's official nationwide tongue, these are now being steadily switched over to Catalan, the preferred language of the Balearic Islands. For the visitor this creates few problems – in many instances English is easily understood, and if you know any Castilian Spanish this remains useful.

In this book, all place-names and streets are in Catalan.

Excursions

Organised coach and minibus excursions are a popular way of seeing the island. If you don't mind travelling at group pace to a pre-ordained itinerary they are an easy way to catch the well-known sights. The choice of routes increases in the summer, when some excursions are combined with a boat trip, for instance from Port de Sóller to Sa Calobra.

Most companies offer set excursions on certain days of the week – they can be booked through your hotel, holiday representative or travel agent. Itineraries do vary, so it pays to shop around. Lunch is sometimes included in the price, but it is rarely anything to get excited about and can devour a lot of sightseeing time. Hotels can provide packed lunches, or

MAJORCA
Majorca is the British name for Mallorca, a term now discouraged by the island authorities. Over the years, helped by the tabloid press and TV sitcoms, the word has gained pejorative connotations. As the Hispanophile Robert Elms put it, Majorca with a hard 'j' has come to mean someone 'wearing an oversize sombrero, carrying a donkey and trailing a family of bad children. The place they are headed is a turbulent ocean of pink flesh and grey concrete.' As this guide hopes to show, Mallorca is somewhere quite different.

you can simply go to a supermarket and create your own picnic.

Favourite destinations for coach tours are Valldemossa, Sa Calobra, the caves at Drac, the pearl factories at Manacor and the country house of La Granja. Trips advertised as an 'Island Tour' are rarely that comprehensive. As a rough guide, excursions venturing into the Serra de Tramuntana or out to Cap de Formentor are the most visually rewarding. It is worth remembering that you can travel under your own steam: Valldemossa is only half an hour's drive or bus ride from Palma, and to travel on the scenic Palma–Sóller train you need just go to the station and buy a ticket.

Viajes Cresta, Carrer de Gremi de Ferrers 48, Palma. Tel: 20 67 12.
Viajes Marsans, Carrer de Catalunya 4, Palma. Tel: 28 51 50.

Take a boat trip from Port de Sóller to Sa Calobra to savour the island's coastline

WHAT TO SEE

'The diligent fuss of a
bootblack in the Borne.
The indifference of the
ticket seller of the little
Sóller railroad.
The unfathomable hurry of
the Mallorcan car driver...
All this is Mallorca, the
island with a thousand
faces.'
JUAN DE LA COSTA
1974

Palma

*P*alma, sometimes referred to simply as Ciutat (City), is the key to Mallorca. Stroll down its leafy promenades, behold the triumphant cathedral, savour the severe façades of its churches and the *joie de vivre* in its art nouveau buildings and you will appreciate the richness of an island that has always been far more than a developers' playground.

PALMA CITY CENTRE

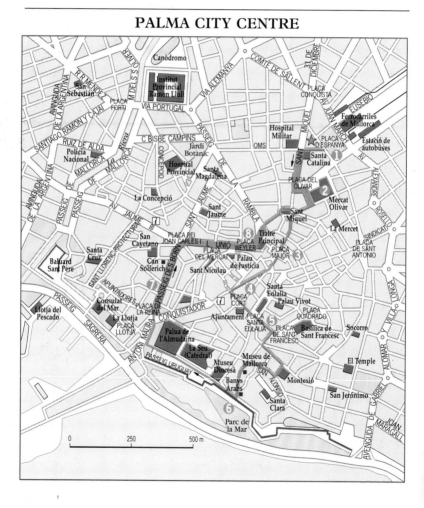

Fishing boats moored along the seafront, watched over by Palma's Gothic cathedral

Palma is a feet-friendly city with its essential sights arranged compactly round a central north–south pedestrian thoroughfare, Passeig des Born. Look at any map and you will see the zigzag shape of the old city walls, now a defensive stream of traffic. Apart from a seafront walk and trips to the Poble Espanyol and Castell de Bellver, there is little need to stray outside these ancient boundaries.

The growth of Palma

The story of present-day Palma begins with the Christian reconquest of the island. Vestiges of the Moorish presence survive in the Banys Àrabs (Arab Baths), but it is the great seafront cathedral, begun in 1230, a year after Jaume I and his troops had taken the island, that puts Palma on the map. A wealth of churches and convents were added in the following centuries (there are still 27

churches within the city walls today), their restrained exteriors complemented by stalwart palaces built by the Mallorcan aristocracy in the 17th and 18th centuries.

By 1900, when Palma's population was some 64,000, the city's outer walls had been demolished and two tree-lined promenades, Passeig de la Rambla and Passeig des Born, built above the original course of Palma's river, La Riera. Today, as part of the Mallorcans' growing respect for their architectural heritage, many of the great turn-of-the-century buildings in the city centre are being restored. The flagship of this renaissance is Palma's Gran Hotel, built in 1902 and reopened in 1993 as the splendid cultural centre, Fundació La Caixa. Palma now has 325,000 citizens, almost half the population of the Balearic Islands, but at its heart it remains a place of peace and civility.

PALMA TOWN PLAN

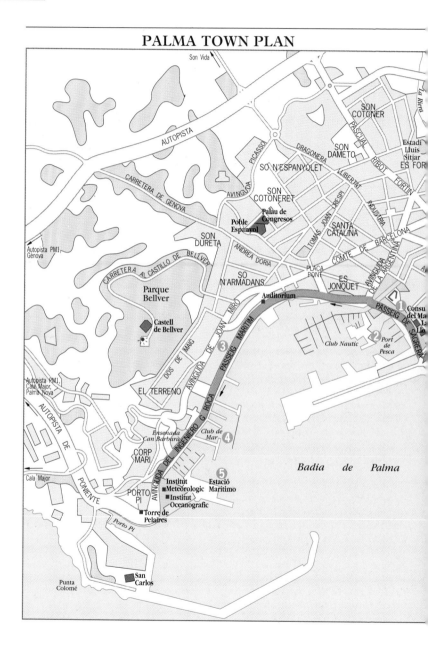

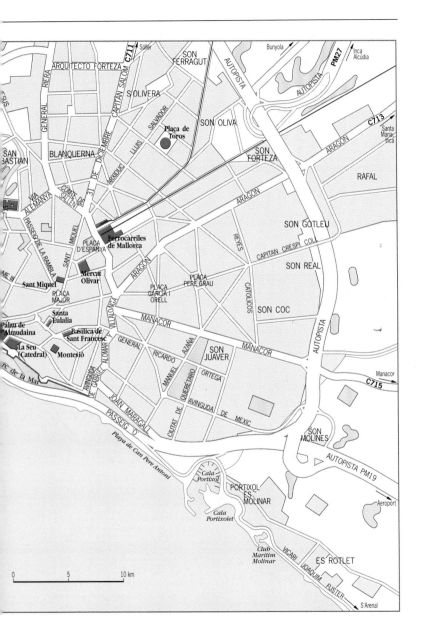

AJUNTAMENT (Town Hall)

Palma's 17th-century town hall is showily grand, as you might expect in a provincial capital, but also charming and clearly citizen-friendly. A long stone bench lines its exterior, where the locals sit looking like an identity parade for the Mallorcan character. Be sure to look up at the long-suffering caryatids and telamons carved in the eaves, and go inside if you happen to be passing when the great doors are open. To the left are a couple of rustic giants used in the city's *fiestas*, and another jolly-faced pair with musical instruments by the central stairs. *Plaça Cort.*

BANYS ÀRABS (Arab Baths)

Tucked away in the claustrophobic streets east of the cathedral, Palma's Arab Baths are an atmospheric souvenir of Medina Mayurqa, the Moorish city that stood here in the 8th to 13th centuries. The baths date from the 10th century: the domed colander-like roof, originally pierced with 25 small skylights, is supported by 12 slender columns. Bathers used to move between two chambers, the hot steamy *caldarium* and the cooler *tepidarium*.

Underneath the arches of the Arab Baths, a legacy of Palma's Moorish occupation

Carrer de Can Serra 3–7. Tel: 72 15 49. Follow the signs from the cathedral. Open: daily in summer 9.30am–8pm (6pm winter). Closed: As it pleases. Admission charge.

BASÍLICA DE SANT FRANCESC

A statue of Junípero Serra, California's founding friar (see pages 36–7), greets visitors to this mighty church. Behind him rises a sober, sunbaked façade with an impressively ornate portal added in 1700. Foundations for the church and monastery of St Francis were laid in 1281, but the original ensemble was remodelled following a strike by lightning in 1580. Visitors now enter through the cloisters, reached through a building to the right (ring the bell). The cloisters are an example of the many tranquil oases that lie hidden behind the high walls of Old Palma. Lemon trees, a central well and arcades of slim Gothic pillars create a meditative ambience. In comparison, the interior of the church, with its vaulted ceiling, baroque altar and intensely decorated side chapels seems pompous and overblown. A focal point of interest is the spot lit tomb of the 13th-century Mallorcan writer Ramón

TOURIST OFFICES

Palma has three tourist offices (*Oficinas de Turísme*). For general information on Mallorca visit the office at Avinguda Jaume III 10 Bajos (tel: 71 22 16). A second office with information on Palma is tucked elusively beneath the eastern end of Carrer de Conquistador at Carrer de Santo Domingo 11 (tel: 72 40 90). There is also a kiosk in Plaça d'Espanya (tel: 71 15 27).

Llull, which is behind the altar in the first chapel on the left. His effigy rests high up in the wall, adorned by an inverted crescent symbolising his missionary work in North Africa.
Plaça Sant Francesc 6–7. Tel: 71 26 95. Open: Monday to Saturday 9.30am–1.30pm and 3.30–7pm. Sunday 9.30am–noon. Closed: Sunday afternoon. Admission charge.

The mighty façade of the Basílica de Sant Francesc conceals restful cloisters

Built to a rare circular design, Castell de Bellver crowns a hill to the west of Palma

CASTELL DE BELLVER
(Bellver Castle)

Even today this great castle, begun in 1309, can easily be seen from Palma's seafront. Framed by thick pinewoods, it stood as a signal to all-comers that the island's rulers were firmly in control. If you do not have a car, consider taking a taxi up, then walking back through the woods – look for the path opposite the entrance, which leads down via a chapel to Carrer de Bellver and Avinguda de Joan Miró.

Bellver means 'good view', and the opportunity to stand on its roof and survey Palma and its bay should not be missed. The castle is remarkable for its circular shape: from the air it looks like a monumental record player. Four round towers stand at the compass points, with the largest, the Tower of Homage,

connected by an arch to the centre. A deep moat, which you can walk right round, completes the defences.

The castle was used as a summer residence by the Mallorcan kings, and served for many centuries as a political prison – graffiti carved by French prisoners-of-war can still be seen on its stones. Today the atmosphere is rather sterile, but the central arcaded courtyard and sweeping stone roof above (carefully designed to feed every raindrop into a central cistern) are aesthetic marvels. Archaeological finds from around Mallorca are exhibited in some of the lower rooms. The castle is used as a venue for concerts in the summer.
West of Avinguda Joan Miró. Tel: 73 06 57. Open: daily April to September 8am–8pm; October to March 8am–6pm. Admission charge.

COLLECCIÓ MARCH
(March Collection)

The Mallorcan banker Joan March, who financed Franco's uprising and became one of the world's wealthiest men, amassed a substantial modern art collection. Among the large and colourful works of Spanish contemporary art displayed here by the Fundació Joan March are ones by well-known names like Picasso, Miró, Dali and the Mallorca-born Miquel Barceló.

Carrer de Sant Miquel 11. Tel: 71 26 01. Open: Monday to Friday 10am–1.30pm and 4.30–7.30pm (5–8pm in winter); Saturday 10am–1.30pm. Closed: Sunday. Admission charge.

FUNDACIÓ LA CAIXA

Palma's Gran Hotel, the city's first quality hotel, opened in 1902. Designed by the Catalan architect Lluis Domènech i Montaner, it was the first of several Modernista (Spanish art nouveau) buildings to grace the city. In 1993, after much loving restoration by the Fundació La Caixa, it was unveiled as a stunning cultural centre staging exhibitions and musical events. Spectacularly lit up at night, it has a popular ground floor bar.

Plaça Weyler 3. Tel: 72 01 11. Open: Tuesday to Saturday 10am–9pm; Sunday 10am–2pm. Closed: Monday. Admission charge for some events.

LA LLOTJA (The Exchange)

Close to the seafront, La Llotja and its adjacent *plaça* (square) and garden are testimony to the maritime might that underpins Palma's prosperity. Built between 1426 and 1456 to designs by Guillem Sagrera, who was also responsible for the cathedral's Portal del Mirador, La Llotja served as a meeting place for the shipping merchants and commercial traders who gathered in the city. A kindly guardian angel hovers over the entrance, but once you are within it is not hard to imagine a cut-throat atmosphere with insider deals being struck on the stone benches and hard-done-by merchants gazing up in despair at the palm-like pillars supporting the vaulted roof. When Palma's seafaring fortunes declined La Llotja became a granary, and it is now used as a venue for cultural exhibitions.

Plaça Llotja. Tel: 71 17 05. Open: Tuesday to Saturday 11am–2pm and 5–9pm; Sunday 11am–2pm. Closed: Monday. Free.

Once a hotel, Fundacío La Caixa is now the flagship of Palma's architectural renaissance

LOCAL HEROES

Mallorca's two best-known sons both gained fame and beatification through their work as missionaries. Ramón Llull, whose flowing-bearded statue enjoys a commanding position on Palma's seafront, was born in 1235 of noble parentage. His sudden conversion to the religious cause is alleged to have been the result of a grotesque incident near Palma's Santa Eulalia church. During a hot-blooded courtship of a married lady, he rode his horse into the church where she was praying, then pursued her down the street. Unable to deter his ardour, his quarry suddenly pulled up her blouse to reveal breasts riddled with cancerous growths.

Duly chastened, the 40-year-old Llull embarked on a career of scholarly devotion that took him to medieval centres of learning around the Mediterranean. A prolific author who wrote in Latin, Catalan and Arabic on subjects ranging from metaphysics to gastronomy, Llull founded a religious sanctuary that still stands on top of Puig de Randa. He is said to have been stoned to death by an infidel mob while spreading the word in Tunisia at the age of 80, and is now buried in the Basílica de Sant Francesc in Palma.

Four centuries later, Junípero Serra (1713–84) was born of humble family in the country town of Petra. At the age of 17 he joined the Franciscan order and in 1749 sailed to Mexico to convert its natives to Catholicism.

When he was 54 Serra embarked on a bold colonising crusade, backed by the Spanish Crown, to establish missionary stations in what is now the state of California. The first was built at San Diego in 1769 and

Homages to Junípero Serra in Palma (above) and Petra

by the time of his death, 15 years later, a line of nine missions stretched north to San Francisco. Twelve more were completed after his death, linked by El Camino Real (The Royal Road).

Mallorca's man of letters, Ramón Llull

PUNISHED FOR PUNS

Two witty heroes of Mallorcan history are portrayed in the Sant Sebastià chapel in La Seu. During the siege of Castell d'Alaró (see page 66) by Alfonsó III in 1285, the soldiers Cabrit and Bassa deliberately mistook the hostile king's name for *anfós*, a local fish. 'We like our *anfós* grilled!' they yelled in defiance. After Alfonsó took the castle, he asked what their names were. Then he roasted Cabrit and Bassa alive on a spit – just like *cabritos* (kid goats).

The Museu Diocesà is packed with curios rescued from the island's religious buildings

MUSEU DE MALLORCA (Museum of Mallorca)

Mallorca's leading historical museum occupies a former palace, Palau de Desbruill, in one of the most atmospheric corners of old Palma. To the right as you enter are rooms devoted to the Moorish occupation of Mallorca, with exhibits that include bowls, jars and pottery oil lamps. In the main building there are rooms devoted to the Talaiotic period (see pages 10–11) with ceramics, Bronze Age tools and weapons, and jewellery. Upstairs, overseen by an attractive angel, are poorly-displayed religious paintings rescued from the island's churches and monasteries, plus painted tiles and crockery from the 18th and 19th centuries. Changing exhibitions on themes like Mallorcan cartography and writers increase the museum's appeal.

Carrer de Portella 5. Tel: 71 75 40. Open: Tuesday to Saturday 10am–2pm and 4–7pm. Sunday 10am–2pm. Closed: Monday. Admission charge.

MUSEU DIOCESÀ (Diocesan Museum)

Tucked round the back of the cathedral in the Episcopal Palace, this is one of the most engaging museums in Palma. More like an antiques shop than a museum, its displays are a wide-ranging mixture of religious and historical *objets trouvés* from around the island, including Roman amphorae, Moorish pottery and painted tiles, Mallorcan coins, bibles, missals and paintings, and statues of pious and suffering saints. Highlights include a 13th-century Mudéjar pulpit, a portrait of Sant Jordi (St George) with medieval Palma in the background and an 18th-century jasper sepulchre for Jaume II. Best of all, you get a rare chance to stare into the eyes of some jovial and anguished religious statues normally set on high.

Carrer de Mirador 5. Tel: 71 40 63. Open: Monday to Friday, April to October 10am–1.30pm and 3–8pm, November to March 10am–1.30pm and 3–6pm. Saturday and Sunday 10am–1.30pm. Admission charge.

MUSEU KREKOVIC (Krekovic Museum)

In the east of the city, this functional purpose-built building is devoted to the romantic paintings of the Croatian artist Kristian Krekovic, who died in 1985. The principal themes are Spanish life and the early civilisations of South America. Although Krekovic's garish-toned style is now unfashionable, his depictions of suffering in Bosnia in the 1940s are depressingly appropriate to more recent conflicts in the former Yugoslavia.

Carrer de Ciutat de Querétaro 3.
Tel: 24 94 09. Bus: 9. Open: Monday to
Friday 9.30am–1.30pm and 3–6pm.
Saturday 9.30am–1.30pm. Closed:
Sunday. Admission charge.

PALAU DE L'ALMUDAINA
(Almudaina Palace)

Almudaina is the Arab word for citadel,
and Palma's Royal Palace evolved from
the Moorish *alcázar* (fortress) that once
commanded the Badia de Palma.
Originally used by the kings of Mallorca,
the palace has had its royal functions
revived with the reinstatement of the
Spanish monarchy, and guided tours
now include visits to the offices used by
King Juan Carlos I and Queen Sofía
when they visit the island in the summer.
Part of the building is still occupied by
the military, who only permit
photography in certain directions.

Tours start in the central courtyard,
and proceed through a series of Gothic
reception rooms and chambers decorated
with antique furniture and tapestries; in
some parts original 17th-century frescos
have been revealed. After walking on the
terrace, where they can enjoy a kingly
view of Palma, visitors return to the
courtyard. On the west side is the Capilla
de Santa Ana, the Royal Chapel, which
has a marbled Romanesque portal and
Gothic nave.
Carrer de Palau Reial. Tel: 71 43 68.
Open: Monday to Friday, June to
September 10am–7pm, October to May
10am–1.30pm and 4–5.30pm. Saturday
10am–1.30pm. Closed: Sunday. Admission
charge but free to EU citizens on
Wednesday.

Palau de l'Almudaina, seat of the Mallorcan
Kings and now the Spanish Royal Family

Take a stroll down the leafy Passeig des Born, Palma's historic promenade

PARC DE LA MAR

Created in the mid-1980s, Parc de la Mar is an extensive multi-level public space bordering the south side of the cathedral. It is worth exploring for the changing vistas it provides of the bay and La Seu, and there are several cafés where you can take a break from the city bustle.

Modern sculpture in the park

includes a tiled mural by Miró, and there is a large lake specifically created to reflect the cathedral. Near here is Ses Voltes, a series of vaults that are now an exhibition and concert space. Further west, on the ramparts and close to a children's playground, is the Arc de la Drassana Musulmana. Looping over a lake with black swans, the arch dates from the Moorish presence in Palma and was once the gateway to the royal docks.

PASSEIG DES BORN

Like Barcelona's Las Ramblas, Palma's Passeig des Born is where city life struts and loiters. In Moorish times it was a moat guarding the walled city, and in Franco's day was inevitably renamed Paseo de Generalissimo Franco. Everyone still called it El Born though, a name derived from its days as a jousting ground.

You will not have 'done' Palma until you have walked 'The Born' or argued with its newspaper-sellers, who are famous for getting upset if you attempt to read a

Is it a bird? Or just another provocative modern sculpture in the Parc de la Mar?

paper before deciding to buy it. Bordered by plane trees, benches and floral urns, and mysteriously guarded by pairs of sphinxes, this pedestrian promenade still functions as a spine dividing the city. At its southern end is Plaça de la Reina and at the north Plaça Rei Joan Carles I, where a bizarre obelisk is supported by four minute tortoises. Near by to the west is the elegant Can Sollerich, an 18th-century palace currently being restored. On the opposite side, Bar Bosch is a focus of city life.

PLAÇA DEL MERCAT

Walk along Carrer de l'Unió to find a popular square that presents a scene typical of traditional Palma. Beneath its venerable rubber tree is a statue of Mallorca's most famous politician, Antoni Maura, who was a conservative prime minister of Spain several times at the start of this century. Behind him rises the belfry of the church of Sant Nicolau. To the left are two vivacious Modernista buildings, the recently restored Pensió Menorquina and next door the rippling Can Casasayas, now a clothes shop. Further along is the Palau de Justícia, Palma's courthouse. It was once a private palace, Can Berga, and you should walk into the courtyard to appreciate the capacious plan on which it was built.

POBLE ESPANYOL (Spanish Village)

Spain in a nutshell is the objective of this architectural theme park-cum-conference facility in the west of Palma. Reproduced attractions include the Patio de los Arrayanes and Arab Baths from Granada's Alhambra, Toledo's mammoth Puerta de Bisagra and Casa de El Greco, a Canary Islands house and an Ayuntamiento (town hall) from

Guipúzcoa. Spain's greatest hits also provide the inspiration for the artefacts in numerous craft workshops and souvenir shops.
Carrer de Poble Espanyol 39. Tel: 73 70 75. Bus: 5. Open: daily 9am–8pm summer; 10am–6pm winter. Admission charge.

SANT MIQUEL

The church of Sant Miquel is one of the most popular in the city. Its plain façade dates from the 14th century. Built on the site of a mosque, it was here that Jaume I celebrated mass after capturing the city in the name of Christianity.
Carrer de Sant Miquel 2. Tel: 71 45 55. Open: Monday to Saturday 8am–1pm and 5–8pm. Sunday as services permit. Admission free.

Spanish architecture's greatest hits are paraded in the Poble Espanyol

La Seu

*B*uilt right on the water's edge for all to see, Palma's cathedral is an expression of political power rather than religious fervour. Like the towering Palau de l'Almudaina and the mighty Castell de Bellver, La Seu was a declaration to the world that the island's Christian colonists were here to stay. It is particularly beautiful when seen from the sea, as intended, but like all great buildings constantly surprises its onlookers. By day the sun burnishes the soft-toned sandstone of its south front; come nightfall its bony skeleton is illuminated like a rocket ship departing for the heavens.

Exterior

Work began on La Seu (the Catalan word for a bishop's see) in 1230, but it was not until 1601 that the cathedral was completed. In 1851 the west front was damaged in an earthquake, and in the restoration two turrets were added and the side rose windows and doors blocked up. The cathedral saves its best profile

The cathedral's south front once stood at the water's edge, now the Parc de la Mar

for the sea, and a stroll along the south front provides good views of the line of pinnacled buttresses that support the central nave. The Portal del Mirador here dates from 1389 and includes a *Last Supper* in the tympanum and five statues on either side of the door by the Mallorcan sculptor, Guillem Sagrera.

Treasury

The cathedral is entered on its north side, through the Portal del Almoina

Detail from the Portal del Mirador (left); gilded relief in the cathedral interior

where alms were dispensed to the poor. This leads into the Treasury, where vast manuscripts, silverware, monstrances, processional props and holy relics are displayed. A pair of early 18th-century man-high candelabra gives a clue to the past wealth enjoyed by the Catholic church in Mallorca.

Interior

Stand with your back to the west front's rarely-opened Portal Mayor, and you will appreciate the size and rhythm of the cathedral's three naves. Supported by 14 slender octagonal pillars, the central nave soars 44m high, and the east rose window, with a diameter of 13.3m, is among the largest in the world. The glass was damaged during an air raid at the start of the Spanish Civil War. In 1902 Antoni Gaudí, architect of Barcelona's dazzling Sagrada Família church, was invited to restore the cathedral to its 14th-century glory. His reforms remain controversial: some visitors will gain spiritual uplift from the illuminated Crown of Thorns now suspended over the altar, others may feel it looks like an accident at a funfair.

Among the 14 side chapels, Nostra Senyora de la Corona (on the south side, second in from the east) has four athletic angels brought from the Carthusian monastery in Valldemossa. Other points of interest are the Plateresque stone pulpit to the north of the altar and the 110 walnut choir stalls carved in 1328. The oldest part of the cathedral, the Trinity Chapel, is behind the altar but not accessible. Inside are the tombs of Jaume II and Jaume III: times have changed since George Sand visited in 1838, when guides would open up their marble sarcophagi so that visitors could behold the mummified corpses. The exit from the cathedral leads through its neglected cloisters. Look up and you can see La Seu's 47m-high bell-tower. When its largest bell, which weighs over 4 tonnes, was rung in 1857 as a storm warning it shattered most of the cathedral's stained glass.

Carrer de Palau Reial 29. Tel: 72 31 30. Open: Monday to Friday April to October 10am–6.30pm; November to March 10am–3pm. Saturday 10am–2.30pm (2pm winter). Museum closed: Sunday. Admission charge.

Historic Palma

This introductory walk reveals the range of atmospheres and vistas hidden in the city's historic streets. It is best done in the morning when the market and churches are open. See map on page 28 for route. *Allow 2 hours, excluding stops at sights and bars.*

Start at Plaça d'Espanya.

1 PLAÇA D'ESPANYA
This is the transport hub of Mallorca. In the centre is an equestrian statue of Jaume I, Conquistador of Mallorca – now reconquered by pigeons.
Walk west via Plaça de la Porta Pintada to Carrer de Sant Miquel. Turn south, past the church of Santa Catalina and the Hospital Militar on the opposite corner.

2 MERCAT OLIVAR
Veer left into Plaça del Olivar to visit the city's most enjoyable market – don't miss the spectacular fish displays in the *pescaderia*.
Take Carrer de Josep Tous I Ferrer back to Carrer de Sant Miquel.

3 PLAÇA MAJOR
Take a look in the church of Sant Miquel (see page 41), then follow the pedestrianised Carrer de Sant Miquel past the Col.Lecció March (see page 35) to reach the enclosed and arcaded Plaça Major, a venue for street entertainers and artisans' stalls. Leave by the opposite arch, then look up to the right to admire two Modernista buildings, L'Àguila and Can Forteza Rei.
Walk down Carrer de Jaume II.

4 PLAÇA CORT
Carrer de Jaume II is typical of the lively

Modernista décor in Carrer de Jaume II

Take a breather in the cafés of Plaça Mayor, a platform for street performers and artisans

pedestrian shopping streets that lie east of Passeig des Born. At the bottom turn left past the blushing edifice of Can Corbella for Plaça Cort. The square, with its wizened olive tree, is dominated by the Ajuntament (see page 32).

Cross to take Carrer del Convent de Sant Francesc.

5 PLAÇA DE SANT FRANCESC

Passing the restored 13th-century church of Santa Eulalia, you reach the Basílica de Sant Francesc (see page 32). The narrow streets around here, with their high-walled, solid-doored buildings, are filled with the introspective spirit of old Palma. Turn back down Carrer del Pare Nadal then left into Carrer de Montesion to reach the Jesuit church of Montesió with its glorious and grimy baroque façade.

Take the adjacent Carrer de Vent, turn right into Carrer de Sant Alonso and Carrer de la Puresa, then go left down Carrer de la Portella. After passing the Museu de Mallorca (see page 38), note the sneering faces adorning the Hostal Isabel II as you leave the old city.

6 PARC DE LA MAR

Sunlight returns as you emerge by the city ramparts. Just before the arching Porta de la Portella, turn right up an incline to walk beside the south front of the cathedral, with views over the Parc de la Mar. At the end descend some steps and turn right into Moorish-style gardens, S'Hort del Rei (see box on page 33).

At the end of the gardens walk through an arch and cross the small garden in Plaça de la Reina.

7 PASSEIG DES BORN

Walk the length of this historic avenue (see page 40).

Turn right into Carrer de l'Unió.

8 PLAÇA WEYLER

Passing the shabby bulk of the Circule de Belles Arts on your left, and the leafy world of Plaça del Mercat (see page 41) on the right, you reach Plaça Weyler and the Modernista grandeur of the Fundació La Caixa (see page 35). Follow the curve of the road, passing the Teatre Principal, to reach the tree-lined avenue of La Rambla – once a river but today awash with flower stalls.

Climb up Costa de la Pols, by the Librería Fondevilas bookshop, to return to Carrer de Sant Miquel.

Maritime Palma

Palma embraces the sea, and a stroll along its waterfront provides ample proof that this long-standing love affair is far from over. This easy walk follows the curve of the bay round from the city centre to its passenger ship terminal, and is particularly enjoyable in the early evening. It can also be done in reverse – just take a taxi, number 1 bus or horse-drawn carriage out to the Estació Marítimo and walk back. (See map on page 30 for route.)
Allow 1½ hours one way.

The walk starts in Passeig de Sagrera, just west of the roundabout and statue of Ramón Llull at the southern end of Avinguda d'Antoni Maura.

1 PASSEIG DE SAGRERA
Lined with tall palms, this pedestrian avenue is flanked to the north by historic buildings recalling Palma's maritime past. An

Working fishing boats add a note of salty realism to the leisured ambience of Palma's seafront

ancient gate to the port, Porta Vella del Moll, has been reconstructed to the left of the 15th-century Exchange, La Llotja (see page 35). Next door is the galleried Consulat del Mar, built in the 17th century as a court to resolve trading disputes. Decorated with flags and cannons, it is now used by the Balearic Islands' government.

Two statues can be seen at either end of Passeig de Sagrera. To the east is the bearded medieval sage Ramón Llull, apparently making notes of traffic violations with pen and quill. To the west is the Nicaraguan writer and modernist poet Rubén Darío.

The main entrance to La Llotja

Cross Avinguda Gabriel Roca by the yellow traffic lights and walk west along the seafront.

2 PORT DE PESCA

Lines of vivid blue nets strung along the quayside mark the entrance to Palma's fishing port, where fishermen paint boats and mend nets. The monumental pair of sundials near by offers a brainteasing explanation of how to convert True Time into Legal Time.

Continue walking west, passing through a small garden.

3 PASSEIG MARÍTIM

Though bordered by a busy road, this waterside promenade allows walkers to progress peacefully round the harbour. A 4.5km cycle track from Portixol west to Sa Pedrera runs alongside. On the left you pass Palma's Reial Club Nautic (Royal Nautical Club), while across the road rise the mighty bastions that once protected Palma. The remains of five windmills dominate the skyline. On the horizon ahead you can see the imposing silhouette of Castell de Bellver. Further along, you reach a tree-lined jetty where

excursion boats offer tours of the harbour, and a monument celebrates Palma's 15th-century cartographers.
Continue west along the seafront.

4 CLUB DE MAR

This walk is really a social climb through Palma's seafaring classes. Hardworking fishing vessels give way to hobby boats and weekend craft, rust buckets and tourist galleons are overshadowed by gin palaces and Mediterranean cruise ships. The Club de Mar is where many of these pleasure boats moor – a captivating sight for anyone drawn to the romance of the sea. Spare a moment to look back across the bay at Palma cathedral.
Follow the pavement east, passing under a bridge.

5 ESTACIÓ MARÍTIMO

Naval ships, cruise liners, ferries from mainland Spain and the other Balearic islands all call here at various times of the year. Walk as far as the large anchor set on a lawn, and you can see two more signs of Palma's maritime prowess: the 15th-century Torre Paraires, like a chess-piece castle, and beyond it the medieval lighthouse at Porto Pi.
Take a taxi or number 1 bus back from Estació Marítimo 2.

West of Palma

*T*he western corner of Mallorca was one of the first areas to be settled by the Spanish in the 13th century – a cross at Santa Ponça commemorates the spot where Jaume I and his troops landed on 12 September 1229. Today a ribbon of resorts decorates the south coast all the way to Sant Telm, the port closest to the dramatic, lizard-shaped island of Sa Dragonera. Inland, and along the precipitous north coast, you can tour some of the most enjoyable mountain scenery on the island.

Scene from the Victory Cross at Santa Ponça

ANDRATX

Known to the Romans as *Andrachium*, Andratx was built inland from its harbour (Port d'Andratx) as a precaution against pirate attack, a measure that has also saved it from the tourism developments now ravaging this coast. Framed by orange groves, the town appears still to be on the defensive with sturdy buildings lining its narrow streets, and its few shops hiding their minimal wares behind opaque doors and curtained windows. Andratx is dominated by the hulking 13th-century church of Santa Maria, rebuilt in the 1720s, and – further up the valley – the castellated 16th-century mansion of Son Mas, currently being restored.
32km west of Palma on the C719.

CASTELL DE BENDINAT

The outline of this 13th-century castle can easily be seen 8km west of Palma, near the turn-off for Bendinat when you are driving along the Palma–Andratx road. Enlarged in the 18th century, Castell de Bendinat is now a conference hall and not open to the public, but nevertheless makes a majestic sight with its battlements, fortified towers and surrounding pinewoods. According to an oft-told story, its name derives from an after-dinner remark uttered by a contented Jaume I after the king and his retinue had dined on the site in 1229. '*Havem ben dinat*' ('We have eaten well'), the monarch declared.

CALA MAJOR

The Badia de Palma is fringed with a string of tourist developments of which Cala Major is the closest to Palma. The resort is a mixture of high class residences now somewhat swamped by mass-market complexes. There is a small sandy beach but parking can be difficult. Further west are two more resorts, **Sant Agusti** and **Ses Illetes**, with similar facilities. The latter has a less frantic atmosphere, with swimming possible off the rocks. The three resorts are fast

becoming one, though who is devouring who is uncertain.

6km west of Palma. Bus: 22. Tourist Office: Carretera Andratx 33, Illetes. Tel: 40 27 39.

The coastline here is dominated by the closely-guarded summer residence of the Spanish Royal Family at Marivent, where the monarchs indulge in their favourite pastimes of sailing and entertaining.

Outside the walls of Castell de Bendinat, now a private conference centre

WEST OF PALMA

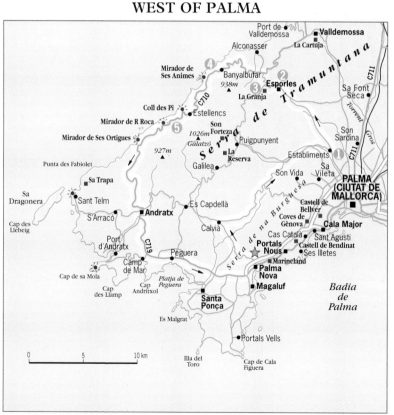

MUSHROOMS

In the Mallorcan countryside you may see signs declaring 'Se Prohibe Buscar Setas' (No Picking Mushrooms). The warnings are worth heeding, not because you might be pinching an islander's breakfast, but because it is hard for the untrained eye to tell the difference between the edible and the poisonous. Some 700 species are found on Mallorca, including four or five that can be deadly. Wild mushrooms are generally picked in the autumn –

look for the trumpet-shaped *girgola* variety sold in markets.

CALVIÀ

On the southern edge of the Serra de Tramuntana, Calvià appears to be just another attractive country town where nothing much happens. But as the administrative centre for the district of Calvià, its municipal offices rule over a great swathe of pulsating resorts stretching west from Ses Illetes to Santa Ponça. Despite the profits and problems this brings, the town remains endearingly tranquil with rustic bars and Mallorcan-cuisine restaurants where you can escape the madness of the coast. Calvià's unmissable landmark is its church, begun in 1245. The small square beside it offers extensive views over the neighbouring farms and fields flecked with olive and carob trees. Don't miss the lively pictorial history of the town displayed in tiles on the wall of the nearby library.
18km west of Palma, take the road to Establiments. Tourist Office: Carrer de Can Vich 29. Tel: 13 91 39.

CAMP DE MAR

In a secluded bay surrounded by high cliffs, this holiday village has a small sandy beach with swimming off the rocks. Just offshore is a tiny islet reached by a frail bridge, where there is a restaurant. An enjoyable 5km walk leads uphill from Camp de Mar, west along a coast of fine views and fragant pines, and down again to Port d'Andratx (see page 56).
25km west of Palma, 4km east of Peguera.

COVES DE GÈNOVA

Nature appears to have created the Coves de Gènova for the convenience of visitors staying in the Palma area. If you don't have the time or inclination to see the great multicoloured caverns at Artà, Drac and Hams (see pages 95, 117 and 120), these caves offer a brief insight into the wonderland of stalactites and stalagmites that lies just below the surface of Mallorca. They are located close to several good restaurants – the entrance is in the grounds of Restaurant Servei and tickets for the guided tour are sold at the bar.
5km west of Palma. Look for signs to Gènova off the Palma–Andratx motorway, then climb up a steep hill to the Coves.

Carrer de Barranc 45. Tel: 40 23 87.
Open: daily 10am–1pm and 4–7pm.
Admission charge.

FUNDACIÓ PILAR I JOAN MIRÓ

In Spanish eyes, the artist Joan Miró is
nothing less than a saint. The hillside
house and purpose-built studio where
the painter lived and worked from 1956
has now been proclaimed 'Miró
Territory'. Galleries have been built in
bleached stone to exhibit some of the
5,000 works he left behind, and you can
peep into the studio where he worked,
left much as it was at his death in 1983.
The adjacent garden, with its trees,
stones and wizened old cartwheel, gives
clues to the way Miró drew inspiration
from the Mallorcan landscape. As his
friend Joan Prats put it: 'When I pick up
a rock it's a rock; when Miró picks it up,
it's a Miró.'

4km from Palma. Bus: 21. Carrer de Joan
de Saridakis 29, Cala Major. Tel: 70 14
20. Open: Tuesday to Saturday 10am–7pm
in summer; 11am–6pm in winter. Sunday
10am–3pm (11am winter). Closed:
Monday. Admission charge with reduction
for EU citizens.

The story of Calvià is recorded in tiles on the
walls of the town library

GALILEA

If you get an urge to jump into a hire car and swap the concrete mayhem of the Badia de Palma for tranquil rural scenery and invigorating mountain air, Galilea would be a worthwhile destination. You can reach this isolated village via Calvià or Puigpunyent (see pages 50 and 58), following winding but generally quiet roads through delightful scenery. To the north rises the mighty peak of Puig de Galatzó.

Surrounded by cultivated hills with almond and carob trees and the odd picturesque windmill, Galilea has developed into an artists' colony. Steep roads lead up to the parish church in Plaça Pio XII, from where there are terrific views down the island to the sea. Two restaurants complement the occasion.

25km west of Palma, 13km north of Calvià.

The mansion of La Granja and its pharmacy

HORT DE PALMA (Garden of Palma)

On the northwestern outskirts of Palma is a fertile area of countryside known as Hort de Palma. This cultivated landscape, with its small villages and undulating roads, is only 5km from the centre of the capital, and makes a refreshing change from the resorts below. Several old estates and mansions have been turned into high-class hotels and restaurants.

From the Palma–Andratx motorway or Via Cintura ringroad, follow the signs north for Son Vida, passing through the busy shopping district of Sa Vileta. The Hotel Son Vida, a converted castle, and the new Arabella Golf Hotel, with gardens and golf courses, are two luxury hotels. Open to non-residents, they make a refined venue for a drink or meal.

LA GRANJA

A grand Mallorcan country house set on a large estate in a wooded valley, La Granja was originally a Cistercian monastery. A natural spring here still spouts water some 9m into the air, and the site has been occupied since Moorish times. Since the 15th century it has been owned by a succession of noble families culminating in its present owners, the Segui family, who take an active interest in running the estate.

La Granja is an engrossing window on Mallorca's past. A vast collection of antiques, furniture, ceramics and art adorn the house, and everyday life on the estate is recalled with displays of tools and household equipment in its kitchens, cellars and workshops. Visitors can watch wool being spun and lace and candles being made, sip Mallorcan wine and herbal liqueurs, and sample traditional home-made cakes and sweets. The bar-restaurant serves tasty Mallorcan dishes. After your meal, you can walk in extensive grounds that include ornamental shrubs, medicinal plants and a 1,200m signposted walk in the company of roaming pigs and goats.

15km northwest of Palma, 1.5km west of Esporles. Tel: 61 00 32. Open: daily 10am–7pm in summer; 9.30am–6pm in winter. Displays of folk music, dancing and games are staged every Wednesday and Friday at 3.30 and 5pm. Admission charge.

LA RESERVA, see page 136.

MARINELAND

The run-of-the-mill resort of Cala d'en Blanes is home to one of the island's best-known family attractions. The stars of Marineland are its performing dolphins and sea lions, whose regular displays of ball-balancing, hoop-jumping, synchronised leaping and zealous aquabatics attract appreciative crowds. In the Parrot Circus trained macaws exhibit their skill at arithmetic and ride a comic cavalcade of bicycles, jeeps and roller skates. Marineland has its serious side too – it boasts one of the largest collections of sharks in Europe, and has bred its own sea lions and dolphins. An aquarium, reptile zoo and pearl diving show are other attractions.

10km west of Palma off the Palma–Andratx motorway. Tel: 67 51 25. Open: daily 9.30am–7.30pm (6pm winter). Closed: 21 November to 26 December. Admission charge.

Performing dolphins are among the many live entertainers at Marineland, Cala d'en Blanes

FLORA

One of the most memorable sights in Mallorca is the pinky-white haze of its almond trees in blossom. Come at the end of January or early in February and the fields of the central plain appear covered with snow. By then the many lemon and orange trees are bejewelled with mature fruit, and Mallorca seems an island of Eden-like plenty.

In March and April wild flowers appear in the banks and verges – tiny orange field marigolds (*Calendula arvenis*) and the tall white-flowered umbellifers and cow parsley known as Queen Anne's lace. On the roadsides you will see shepherd's purse (*Capsella bursa-pastoris*), common fennel (*Foeniculum vulgare)*, bright yellow oxalis and the white flowers of the tall, spiky asphodel. Walkers will enjoy the blue-flowered rosemary and vivid

Spring blossoms in a country garden (left);
oranges, almonds and lemons (below);
coastal flowers (right)

yellow broom that illuminate the hills.

The shiny-leaved strawberry tree
(*Arbutus unedo*), with fruits that turn red
in October, always draws the attention –
there are plenty on the road between Can

Picafort and
Artà. Carob
trees, holm
oaks, dwarf
palms and
Aleppo pines
are ubiquitous,
as are silvery-
leaved olive
trees. Some
of these are
over 1,000
years old with fantastically contorted
trunks to prove it. At dusk, as George
Sand noted, they resemble fairy-tale
monsters 'which one expects every
moment to break into prophetic voice'.

With such natural abundance, the
Mallorcans are understandably fond of

flowers. Take a walk through the flower
stalls on Palma's La Rambla and you
can see the serious contemplation that
invariably precedes a purchase. Like
their Moorish predecessors, the
islanders value gardens as places of
beauty and refuge from the summer
heat. Their balconies and patios are
often full of ferns, carnations and
geraniums, and in the resorts garish
modern architecture is tempered by the
presence of date palms, cacti,
honeysuckle and bougainvillaea.

PALMA NOVA

The gaudy, throbbing heart of mass tourism on the island, Palma Nova offers the archetypal package holiday experience. The beach here is good, with fine white sands somewhere under the rows of bronzing bodies, and shallow, children-safe water near by. Behind this lies a dense grid of high-rise apartment blocks and hotels with plenty of bars, restaurants and souvenir shops. A five-minute walk inland, in Carrer de Tenis, is the family amusement Golf Fantasia.

To the west, Palma Nova merges into **Magaluf**, creating a continuous resort sometimes referred to as Maganova. Magaluf was among Mallorca's earliest tourist developments and is synonymous with the cheap 'n' cheerful sun 'n' sea holidays that brought the island to the world's attention – though not always for the right reasons. Magaluf is still a concrete jungle, and still attracts a raucous element, but work is underway to give both resorts an overdue facelift, widening the seafront promenade and creating new boulevards, gardens and green spaces.

14km west of Palma off the Palma–Andratx motorway. Tourist Office: Avinguda Magaluf. Tel: 13 11 26.

PEGUERA

Peguera is a well-established package holiday centre with two sandy beaches, Platja de Palmira and the smaller Platja de Tora. Several of its hotels stay open through the winter, and the resort is particularly popular with British visitors. The recent opening of a by-pass and tunnel diverting traffic to the north of the town, and the construction of a new seafront promenade and extended beach, should enhance Peguera's appeal.

21km west of Palma on the C719. Tourist Office: Plaça Aparcaments. Tel: 68 70 03.

PORT D'ANDRATX

Exploiting a deep natural harbour, Port d'Andratx is a classic example of a pretty fishing port turned upmarket holiday resort. The old harbour on the east side of the bay has charm and agreeable fish restaurants, while to the west lie the Club de Mar and a parade of luxury villas climbing up the hillside. The port is a favourite haunt of the yachting set. In summer boat excursions run to the nearby island of Sa Dragonera (see pages 138–9).

35km west of Palma, 5km south of Andratx.

Take a stroll around the harbour at Port d'Andratx, well-known to the yachting set

Porto Portals, where the rich moor up

PORTALS NOUS
Portals Nous is an upmarket tourist complex with a small sandy beach and swimming off the rocks. At its eastern end is Porto Portals, a top-notch marina opened in 1987 that attracts fabulously expensive yachts and cruisers. If you like to mix with the well-tanned well-off, and enjoy promenading past ship's chandlers and boutiques selling designer nautical gear, this is the place for you. There is a good choice of ritzy restaurants with cuisine ranging from nouvelle to Chinese. Behind this opulent shore, high-walled villas sit among the pines, and barking dogs warn that you are on moneyed ground.

10km west of Palma off the PM1 motorway.

PORTALS VELLS

A left turn off the Palma–Andratx road, signposted Cala Figuera, leads south past a golf course and thick pinewoods to the western horn of the Badia de Palma. A turning left down a dusty side road can take you to the tiny but official nudist beach at **Platja Mago**, where there is a small beach bar.

Continuing south you reach the small bay of Cala de Portals Vells. Walk along the south side of the cliffs and you will reach the **Cove de la Mare de Déu**, a rock church with two altars and elaborate rock carvings. Legend has it that Genoese fishermen sheltering from a storm placed a statue of the Virgin from their ship in the caves as a thanks-offering for their survival. In 1866 the statue was taken to the chapel on the seafront in Portals Nous. In the 13th and 14th centuries the caves were quarried to supply stone for Palma cathedral. The peninsula is also used by the military.
24km southwest of Palma.

PUIGPUNYENT

Tucked in a valley, Puigpunyent is a pretty village you will inevitably pass through if you are touring the interior of the western Serra de Tramuntana. Near by are the historic country house of La Granja, the splendid nature reserve La Reserva, and the epic road to Galilea (see pages 52–3 and 136). Two kilometres along the road north to Esporles is the 17th-century mansion house of Son Forteza, a typical Mallorcan country residence with waterfalls and citrus orchards. Only the gardens are open to the public, on an irregular basis, and you may be able to purchase some of the fruit grown on the estate.
15km northwest of Palma, 8km west of Establiments.

SANTA PONÇA

Just west of the Badia de Palma, this sheltered resort enjoys an attractive site with pinewoods and a large sandy beach washed by clear, shallow water. Often used by British tour operators, it gets packed out in summer but never attains the brash atmosphere of nearby Magaluf. A marina, golf course and watersports are part of its wide-ranging facilities.

Caleta de Santa Ponça

From the marina a road signposted Sa Caleta leads south to the rocky headland

THE CONQUEST OF MALLORCA

Jaume I's original plan was to land his troops in the Badia de Pollença, but a storm forced his fleet along the island's north coast to Sant Telm. He came well armed, with 150 ships carrying 16,000 troops and 1,500 horses. The Moors fled to the mountains, and Palma was besieged for three months before its surrender on 31 December 1229. By the following March, the king was rewarding his *conquistadores* with huge estates

of Es Malgrat. *En route* you will reach a superb vantage point, Caleta de Santa Ponça, where there is a large white Victory Cross. The memorial was erected in 1929 to commemorate the 700th anniversary of the landing on Mallorca of Jaume I of Aragón on 12 September 1229. In the battle that morning some 1,500 Moors were killed – sculpted scenes depict the bravery of the Christian troops.

Further along the same road, after passing many substantial villas, there is another panoramic viewpoint where you can enjoy the sea air and look back to Santa Ponça. Fishermen appear to enjoy coming to this spot to sit perilously on the cliff-edge with their long rods. Out to sea lie the craggy islands of Illa Malgrat and Illa na Fordada, and further west the headlands of Cap Andritxol and Cap des Llamp.

Left: monument, Santa Ponça
Below: Santa Ponça's marina

20km west of Palma on the C719. Tourist Office: Puig de Galatzó. Tel: 68 70 03.

West of Palma

You do not have to drive far from Palma or its neighbouring resorts to enjoy the peace and beauty of Mallorca's countryside. This 86km circular trip guides you round the mountains to the northwest of Palma, climbing along winding rural roads to reach the spectacular cliffs and sea views of the north coast. See page 49 for route. *Allow 5 hours.*

The tour begins at Palma Nova, 5km west of Palma on the PM1 motorway or C719.

1 ESTABLIMENTS

Take the PM1015 north, following signs to Calvià. The highrise buildings of the coast are soon replaced by woods and well-tended farmland, and the twin spires of Calvià's church can be seen in the distance. In the centre of this town (see page 50), turn right at a T-junction in the direction of Establiments. Climbing steadily, you pass several grand country houses with wrought-iron gates guarding their entrances. The small village of Establiments is where George Sand and Chopin first stayed during their visit of 1838–9, amid a landscape she considered worthy of Poussin's paintbrush.

From Establiments take the left turn to Esporles.

Terrace view:
working the fields in
Banyalbufar

2 ESPORLES

Sheltered by high mountain ridges, this pretty town of tree-lined streets makes a pleasant place to stop for a drink or lunch. Apples, pears, oranges and figs, grown on the terraces surrounding Esporles, are sold in its shops.
Continue north following the signs to Banyalbufar and La Granja.

3 LA GRANJA

La Granja offers a rare chance to get inside one of the highly covetable *fincas* (country houses) that adorn the interior of Mallorca. Today it is a folk museum (see page 53).
Continue north to join the C710, turning left for Banyalbufar.

4 BANYALBUFAR

The sinuous drive along this coast provides magnificent views of mountains, terraced slopes, high cliffs and the sea far below. Clinging perilously to a narrow ridge is the small village of Banyalbufar – some of the buildings lining its narrow main street are supported by stilts. A few shops and hotels cater to visitors seeking an away-from-it-all holiday. A steep, winding road leads down to the tiny port.
Continue west through Estellencs.

5 MIRADORES

The steep terraces along here, which support thriving crops of tomatoes, grapes and flowers, were originally constructed by the Moors and are still worked mostly by hand. Several viewpoints (*miradores*) provide a chance to stop and take in the impressive coastline. The first, Mirador de Ses Animes, has a restored watchtower built on a high rock beside the cliffs (which can be climbed). If this is crowded, you can continue on through Estellencs to a

Coastal watchtower at the Mirador de Ses Animes (Souls), just south of Banyalbufar

second *mirador* at Coll des Pi. Here there are refreshments and a petrol station, and a good view inland to Puig de Galatzó (1,026m).

Estellencs has a parish church dating from 1422, and a tortuous road leads down to a small cove with a rocky beach. Further southwest are more viewpoints, Mirador de Ricardo Roca, which has a large restaurant, and Mirador de Ses Ortigues.
The road descends comfortably through fields studded with olives to the stately old town of Andratx (see page 48). A 5km detour can be made from here down to Port d'Andratx, where there is a good choice of harbourside restaurants (see page 56). From Andratx it is a simple 13km drive east along the fast C719 to Palma Nova.

Sa Trapa

Hidden away in the cliffs north of Sant Telm, the abandoned Trappist monastery of Sa Trapa will linger long in the minds of anyone who makes the effort to get there. The best route provides superb views over the island of Sa Dragonera, but involves some scrambling up steep rocks. If you prefer, you can go and return by an inland cart track, as the monks surely did. Take a light picnic.
Allow 3 hours return, excluding time at Sa Trapa.

The small resort of Sant Telm lies 8km west of Andratx and is connected by bus to Palma via Peguera. There is a frequent service to Andratx, and you can take a taxi to Sant Telm from the rank beside the Teatro Argentino there. If you are driving, park by the start of the walk at the northern end of Sant Telm in Plaça de Mosser Sebastià Grau – where there is a blue and white windmill.

1 SANT TELM

Follow the shore along Avinguda Jaume I and Carrer Cala en Basset bearing right into Plaça de Mosser Sebastià Grau. Take Avinguda de la Trapa inland, which becomes a country track

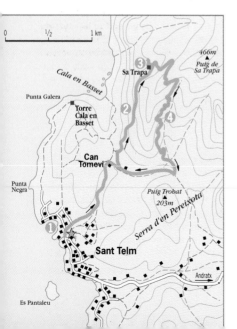

through pinewoods to a farmhouse named Can Tomeví. Here a sign directs you right for Sa Trapa, passing behind the house. At the next sign, Sa Font des Mores, you have a choice – turn left for a steep ascent of the cliffs, or continue straight on to follow the easier but longer inland track up to Sa Trapa (380m) – also the return route.

2 THE ASCENT

Turning left, walk through the woods until you reach a pair of small concrete gateposts. Turn right here, marked on a nearby stone by the first of many intermittent black paint arrows that lead the way. The path narrows as it climbs through the trees, crossing several walls and passing the stone ruins of a limekiln. Eventually you ascend above the pines, with ever-improving views of craggy Sa

Monastery with a view: the island of Sa Dragonera as seen from the ascent to Sa Trapa

Dragonera just offshore. After a short scramble up through dwarf palms and over steep, bare rocks, you will meet a well-established path that makes an ascending run north through the trees.

Passing a '280' in blue paint, you reach a clifftop viewpoint – a good place to take a breather and admire the coastline below. Continue to follow the path as marked, taking care on the final ascent which nears the cliff-edge – heed the warning crosses and veer right. Suddenly you are on top of the promontory and can see the romantic buildings of Sa Trapa in the valley ahead.

3 SA TRAPA

Follow the path to the monastery, a formidable ensemble where you can wander round the ruined chapel, kitchen and living quarters. Almond trees continue to blossom on its perfectly-built terraces, the mill still has its ancient machinery and you can easily make out the wide sweep of the threshing floor, now punctured by pines that have grown up since the monastery's closure in the late 18th century. A memorial stone near by is a sad reminder to keep away from the cliff-edge here.

4 THE DESCENT

Sa Trapa is now being restored and conserved by the Grupo Ornithologia Balear (GOB) and the track used by their vehicles offers an easy descent. This leads inland from behind the monastery, climbs over a pass, then winds patiently down the mountainside providing ample time to dwell upon the life of this isolated Trappist community. At the bottom the track crosses a bridge, curves through a farm and – forking right – leads down to the house at Can Tomeví.

The Northwest

Served by Mallorca's two railway lines, this is both the most accessible part of the island and the best place to get a taste of Mallorca as it was before the resorts arrived. Besides being a spectacular mountain range, the Serra de Tramuntana is full of secrets. Take the slow train up to Sóller, make the hairy descent to Sa Calobra, pay a visit to the monasteries at Valldemossa and Lluc and you will have a completely different image of Mallorca.

ALFABIA

The gardens of Alfabia are a delightful memento of the days when Mallorca was under Moorish rule. Then the estate was known as Al-Fabi ('jar of olives' in Arabic), a lofty residence fit for viziers (high-ranking officials) where the Arab talent for irrigation, garden design and horticulture flourished. Though sadly neglected now (efforts are being made at restoration), the estate remains an inviting oasis where you can spend a dreamy morning or afternoon in the shade of swaying palms and fragrant flowers.

An avenue of magisterial plane trees guides visitors to the stone archway marking the entrance. Follow the directions to walk to the left of the house

and up steps to the gardens. Cobbled paths lead past a huge cistern and water channels to a long pergola wreathed with a colourful mix of bignonia, bougainvillaea, wistaria and honeysuckle. Lavender, sage and box form low hedges, while tall date palms and exotic shrubs provide shaded walks accompanied by the soothing tune of flowing water. At a lower level there are ponds with lilies and fish, bamboos, twining subtropical plants and groves of lemon and orange trees in side gardens.

The house, though somewhat run-down, is a fascinating relic of bygone

The house and gardens at Alfabia, a retreat from the summer heat since Moorish times

THE NORTHWEST

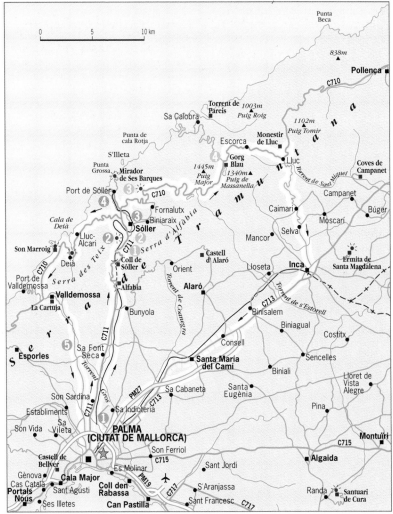

0   5   10 km

Punta
Beca

838m

Pollença

C710

Punta de
cala Rotja

Sa Calobra

Torrent de   1003m
Pareis   Puig Roig

1102m
Puig Tomir

Escorca   Monestir
             de Lluc

S'Illeta

Punta
Grossa

Mirador
de Ses Barques

Gorg
Blau

1445m
Puig
Major

1340m
Puig de
Massanella

Lluc

Coves de
Campanet

Torrent de Sant Miquel

Port de Sóller

C710

Fornalutx

Biniaraix

Campanet

Caimari

Búger

Moscari

Cala de
Deià

Sóller

Selva

Son Marroig

Lluc-
Alcari

Serra d'Alfàbia

Mancor

Deià

Coll de
Sóller

Castell
d'Alaró

Ermita de
Santa Magdalena

Orient

Lloseta

Inca

Port de
Valldemossa

C710

Serra des Teix

Alfàbia

Alaró

C713

Torrent de s'Estorell

Valldemossa

La Cartuja

Bunyola

Torrent de Coanegra

Binisalem

Biniagual

Costitx

Esporles

Sa Font
Seca

C711

Consell

Sencelles

Son Sardina

Torrent Gros

PM27

C713

Santa María
del Camí

Biniali

Lloret de
Vista
Alegre

Establiments

Sa
Vileta

C711

Sa Indioteria

Sa Cabaneta

Santa
Eugènia

Pina

Son Vida

PALMA
(CIUTAT DE MALLORCA)

Castell de
Bellver

Son Ferriol

Es Molinar

C715

Sant Jordi

Algaida

C715

Montuïri

Gènova

Cala Major

Cas Català

Portals
Nous

Sant Agustí

Coll den
Rabassa

PM19

Ses Illetes

Can Pastilla

S'Aranjassa

Sant Francesc

C717

Randa

Santuari
de Cura

days with faded wall panels and antique furniture – look out for the 14th-century carved wooden chair and an ancient cradle.

14km north of Palma on the C711 to Sóller. Tel: 61 31 23. Open: Monday to Saturday 9.30am–7pm (5.30pm November to March). Closed: Sunday. Admission charge.

BINISALEM

Binisalem is the centre of Mallorca's wine-making industry. Viticulture was introduced to the islands by the Romans and survived the Moorish occupation (Binisalem means 'House of Salem' in Arabic). Production reached a peak in the late 19th century when blight struck the French vineyards. Then there were 30,000 hectares under vines; today it is down to 300, but the reputation of Mallorcan wines is growing with the help of modern technology and grape varieties exclusive to the island. Wine can be bought from the Bodega José Ferrer (minimum purchase six bottles). For El Foro de Mallorca wax museum, see page 159.

22km northeast of Palma on the C713.

The island's best wine comes from Binisalem

CASTELL D'ALARÓ

There is little reason to linger in the village of Alaró, except on a Friday afternoon when you might buy picnic provisions in the market prior to ascending to the nearby Castell d'Alaró (817m). To reach this romantically-sited castle drive northeast on the PM210 towards Orient. At km18 a turning left leads on to a narrow road bordered by stone walls and fields of olives and almond trees. This degenerates into a rough dirt track full of potholes and best suited to four-wheel drive vehicles or hikers with sturdy footwear.

An alternative approach is to continue skirting right round Puig d'Alaró, park near km11, then follow a path up through the terraces. Either way, you eventually reach a high plateau where your perseverance is rewarded with fantastic views and Es Pouet, a rustic bar-restaurant that serves delicious roast lamb cooked in a clay oven. From here you must walk (30 minutes) up steep and winding stone steps to see the ruins of the 15th-century castle. A small chapel, Mare de Déu del Refugi, has stood here since 1622 and a hostelry still offers sanctuary to pilgrims and visitors.

29km northeast of Palma, 6km north of Alaró.

COSTITX

Typical of the many small towns in the interior of Mallorca, Costitx was the main centre of population on the island in prehistoric times, and the area has proved a rich source of archaeological treasure. The 14th-century image of the Virgin in its parish church is said to have been found by children in an apple tree.

Casa de Sa Fauna Ibero-Balear

On the south side of the main road from

The subterranean caves at Campanet, coloured with fancy names and lights

spectacular as those at Artà, Drac or Hams (see pages 95, 117 and 120), but neither are they as crowded with visitors. The well-signposted entrance is through a colourful garden dripping with bougainvillaea and other flamboyant plants, and a large terrace provides a rewarding opportunity to sit with a drink and survey the charming rural scenery in the Sant Miquel valley.

Conducted tours lead visitors into a subterranean maze that winds for some 1,300m, past colourfully illuminated stalactites and stalagmites and 'The Enchanted Town'.

41km northeast of Palma, 12km northwest of Inca. Tel: 51 61 30. Open: daily 10am–7.30pm (5pm in winter). Admission charge.

Costitx to Sencelles, signposted Casa Cultura, this modern building exhibits stuffed and preserved examples of the fauna of the Balearic Islands, including wild birds, fish and butterflies. There is a bar-restaurant and library, and a good view of the surrounding agricultural plains.

Can Font. Tel: 51 31 98. Open: daily 9.30am–1pm and 6–9pm (3–7pm in winter). Admission charge.

24km northeast of Palma, 4.5km east of Sencelles.

COVES DE CAMPANET

Campanet is a quiet old town, devoid of tourism and peaceful even on market day. Just 3km to the north though, the Coves de Campanet are a magnet for sightseers and excursion coaches. Discovered in 1945, the caves are not as

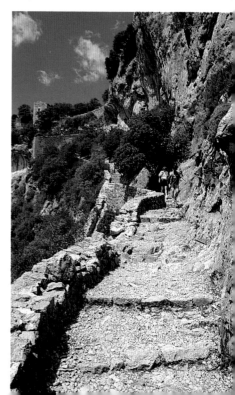

The path up to the ruins of the 15th-century Castell d'Alaró, fine views guaranteed

Deià: a Mediterranean dream village where the poet Robert Graves set up home in 1929

ROBERT GRAVES

The English poet and novelist Robert Graves (1895–1985) is well known for his two bestsellers: *Goodbye to All That,* an autobiographical account of his experiences in World War I, and *I, Claudius*, a historical novel that brings to life ancient Rome. Money made from the first book enabled him to move to Mallorca with his muse, mistress and fellow poet Laura Riding. After World War II he settled permanently on the island, writing fiction, poetry and books on mythology.

DEIÀ

Lodged amid the mountains of the north coast, Deià will be forever associated with the English writer Robert Graves, who came to live here in 1929 and developed a deep affection for Mallorca and its people. He is buried in the cemetery beside the parish church at the top of the town. Graves strove hard to stop Deià being ruined by the encroaching tourist developments, and the town's unified and natural appearance is its greatest attraction. There are several restaurants, a couple of art galleries, and a narrow, twisting road that leads down to the sea at Cala de Deià.

Deià and its environs has a good proportion of foreign residents, though rising property prices have changed the atmosphere. Today the town lives in thrall to La Residencia, an idyllic mansion turned hotel that is partly owned by the British entrepreneur Richard Branson and attracts arty types from around the world. As the author Robert Elms put it, 'Everything in Deià is taken slowly, except your money.' *30km north of Palma, 4km south of Lluc-Alcari.*

FORNALUTX

This is a truly pretty mountain village with a narrow cobbled high street that twists round to a tiny square. The church dates from 1680. Several cafés and inviting restaurants, such as the Santa Marta with its terrace views, make Fornalutx a welcome goal if you are walking from Sóller. Follow the rural

road east via Biniaraix, through a valley graced with orange and lemon groves.
40km north of Palma, 8km northeast of Sóller via the C710 to Lluc or 5km via Biniaraix.

INCA

At the end of the railway line from Palma, this modern industrial town is heavily promoted as a place all tourists should visit. Excursions are arranged to the Thursday outdoor market, which spreads around the streets bordering the covered daily market, and usually include a visit to one of the town's several leather factories or their retail outlets along Avinguda General Luque and Gran Via de Colon. Prices are not so low as to merit a special trip, but there is plenty of choice.

Pursuers of Mallorcan cuisine will appreciate the *celler* restaurants in the town centre, where the wine is extracted from mammoth vats and you can join the locals devouring local specialities like *caracoles* (snails) and roast suckling pig. Can Amer in Carrer den Miquel Durán is a famous example. In the shops you may see *concos d'Inca* ('Inca bachelors') for sale, a type of cake made by the nuns of Monasterio de las Jerónimas. The island's top agricultural show is held here on the third Thursday in November and is known as *Dijous Bò* – Good Thursday.

Ermita de Santa Magdalena

A turning right off the Inca–Alcúdia road leads up to Puig d'Inca (304m) and a small sanctuary offering far-reaching views over the countryside and mountains. There is a small chapel and a café. A pilgrimage, said to have been followed for 800 years, is made every year to the *ermita* on the first Sunday after Easter.

30km northeast of Palma on the C713.

The gentle central square in Fornalutx, a mountain village surrounded by citrus groves

CREATIVE MALLORCA

Mallorca has stimulated the creativity of many visiting writers, musicians and artists. George Sand was convinced that the sublimity of Chopin's *Preludes,* composed or completed during their stay at Valldemossa in 1838–9, was a direct response to an environment enriched by deceased monks, birds singing in wet trees, and the twang of far-off guitars. To her mind, raindrops falling on the Charterhouse roof were transformed by Chopin's 'imagination and singing gift into tears falling on the heart'. Chopin denied that his art was achieved by a puerile imitation of the external, but critics agree that he emerged from his Mallorcan sojourn a maturer composer.

The painter and sculptor Joan Miró, whose mother and wife came from Mallorca, was more candid about the direct influence of the island on his vibrantly-coloured work. 'As a child,' he recalled, 'I loved to watch the always changing Mallorcan sky. At night I would get carried away by the writing in the sky of the shooting stars, and the lights of the fireflies. The sea, day and night, was always blue. It was here that I received the first creative seeds which became my work.' Miró's studio on the outskirts of Palma is a testimony to the way the artist found inspiration in nature's little works – a piece of driftwood, an almond stone, a dry-stone wall 'carved by real masters'.

The minutiae of island life also absorbed the writer and long-term Deià-resident Robert Graves, whose *Majorcan Stories* chronicle tragicomic vicissitudes befalling both locals and visitors, such as the theft of a bicycle or a farcical christening.

The greatest and most diligent creative response to Mallorca, however, must be the work of the indefatigable Archduke Luis Salvador. Arriving on the island in 1867, at the age of 19, he sank his fortune into

Joan Miró
at work

A fresh rose always rests on Chopin's piano in Valldemossa, where the composer stayed

researching his beloved island, sponsoring investigations of its caves and archaeological sites and producing a comprehensive six-volume study of the Balearic Islands, *Die Balearen,* that is still valued to this day.

The monastery at Lluc has grown from humble 13th-century origins into a monumental complex

LLUC

A revered place of pilgrimage since its founding in 1250, the Monestir de Lluc (Monastery of Lluc) is a testimony to the Mallorcans' continuing religious conviction. Legend has it that a shepherd boy discovered an image of a dark-skinned Virgin in the forest here and took it to the local priest. The Virgin was placed in the village church at Escorca, but disappeared three times, always being found in the same spot in the forest. Taking this as a divine command, the priest ordered the construction of a chapel to house the peripatetic Virgin.

Today Lluc is a colossal ensemble that includes a church, choir school, the old Augustinian monastery, a small museum, accommodation for pilgrims and a restaurant and souvenir shop for visitors. To reach the church, enter the main building by the front portal, following a short passage past a patio with a magnificent magnolia to a courtyard. To the right is the baroque façade of the church. Inside, steps lead up behind the altar to a chapel and the jewel-adorned image of La Moreneta, the Little Dark One, who is Mallorca's patron saint. You can hear the choirboys – known as Els Blavets (The Blues) from the colour of their cassocks – at the 11.15am service. The museum, on the first floor, contains an engaging miscellany of thanksgiving gifts, archaeological finds, coins, costumes and paintings. To the left of the monastery buildings is a path leading to a Way of the Cross, with good views of the quiet countryside. The sculptures, depicting the Mysteries of the Rosary, are the work of the Modernista architects Antoni Gaudí and Joan Rubió, who also carried out modernisations to the church at Lluc. Several mountain walks start from here.

47km northeast of Palma, 16km north of Inca. Tel: 51 70 25. Open: daily 10am–7pm (till 5.30pm in winter). Admission charge for museum.

ORIENT

Claiming to be the smallest village on the island, and once a classic example of

'hidden Mallorca', Orient is now being discovered. The official population is 26, but at weekends this can swell to 300 when trippers from Palma come up for an away-from-it-all lunch in the countryside. Take the road (PM210) east from Bunyola, a twisting, taxing drive with a fine view at every bend. Inaccessibility keeps Orient free of tourist coaches, and its cluster of white houses snuggles beside the mountains of the Serra d'Alfàbia in picture-book style. The village now has a luxury hotel, L'Hermitage, which occupies the country seat of a 17th-century Spanish Duke, and a *hostal* offering accommodation and food for the many walkers who pass through. You can climb up to Castell d'Alaró from here (see page 66).
25km north of Palma on the Bunyola–Alaró road.

L'Hermitage in Orient: a country house hotel offering luxury and Mallorcan antiques

PORT DE SÓLLER

A quiet and sheltered resort popular with French visitors, Port de Sóller was once the main outlet for produce grown in the valleys and terraces around Sóller. A long, curving seafront bordered by shops and restaurants caters to the daily influx of trippers arriving on the historic tram that connects the port to Sóller (see page 75). There is a small sandy beach to the south of the bay that allows swimming. Other attractions are the boat trips along the north coast, particularly to Sa Calobra (see page 74), and the walk up to the lighthouse and Punta de Sóller (see pages 86–7).
40km north of Palma, 5km north of Sóller. Tourist Office: Carrer de Canónigo Oliver. Tel: 63 01 01.

Port de Sóller: once a main outlet for island produce, now importing tourists

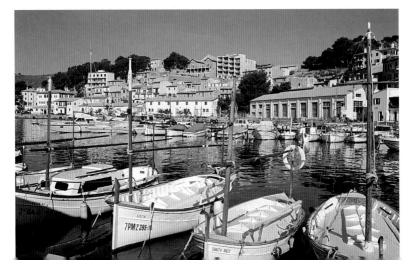

Sea-view through a rock arch at Sa Calobra, for some the highlight of their visit

SA CALOBRA

Eavesdrop on the didn't-we-do-well conversations of holidaymakers returning from Mallorca, and it is not long before someone mentions Sa Calobra. Previously remote and only accessible by boat, Sa Calobra is a tiny, once-idyllic cove at the bottom of sheer cliffs near Escorca. It can now be reached by a snaking road that is at least as interesting as the cove itself: there are countless hairy hairpins, a looping flourish of road engineering known as Nus de la Corbeta (the Knotted Tie), and plenty of chances to inspect the dramatically eroded limestone cliffs that are home to disdainful seabirds and tenacious alpine flowers. If you are driving, expect to have to reverse when you meet a coach.

Near the end of the road is a new holiday development, Cala Tuent, and down by the sea a car park and bars where dazed visitors can recover. The next challenge is to walk through a set of dimly lit tunnels cut in the rock, with some stooping required, to reach the Torrent de Pareis. Formed over thousands of years by water rushing down from the Serra de Tramuntana, this gorge culminates in a small sandy beach – a great picnic spot if you could

Do the twist on the road down to Sa Calobra, or take a boat trip from Port de Sóller

make the crowds disappear. The gorge has two splendid waterfalls and is only 30m wide with walls rising up to 608m. As the guides cannot resist saying: 'Welcome to Mallorca's Grand Canyon.'
67km north of Palma, 16km northwest of Escorca.

SANTA MARIA DEL CAMÍ
Santa Maria is a historic market town with some notable old buildings. In Plaça Caidos stands the 18th-century church of Santa Maria with its bell-tower decorated with deep blue tiles. Inside is a painting of the Madonna and baby Jesus, who is holding a goldfinch. Signposts direct visitors to the mighty 17th-century Convent dels Mínims on the C713. The ground floors of the former convent are now a *bodega* (wine bar), where you can taste and buy wines and spirits made on the island.

Next door is a leather factory and shop, and a private historical museum, Can Conrado (Conrado House Collection) – open 4–7pm; closed Sunday).
14km northeast of Palma on the C713.

SÓLLER
Whether you approach Sóller by road, crossing the mountain pass at Coll de Sóller, or arrive on the old-world train from Palma (see pages 82–3), this affable town makes a memorable impression. Sprinkled across the broad fertile Valle de los Naranjos (Valley of the Oranges), Sóller is still redolent of the turn-of-the-century days when its citizens grew prosperous from the citrus fruit trade.

Plaça Constitució
Take a seat in Sóller's central square, with its venerable trees and fountains, and it is not hard to imagine the

Small town style: the Modernista Banco de Sóller in Sóller's Plaça Constitució

excitement and pride which must have greeted the opening of the railway line to Palma in 1912, and of the rickety tram line down to Port de Sóller the following year. Look up at the ostentatious Modernista façades of the Banco de Sóller and church of Sant Bartomeu next door, and you see the strange fruits of the vagaries of the fruit business. In the 1860s the orange groves were struck by blight, and many of Sóller's residents were forced to seek their fortunes elsewhere. Those that succeeded returned home with new, fanciful ideas from abroad. Examples are these buildings by Joan Rubió, a pupil of Gaudí, who also created a fluid art nouveau mansion, Can Prunera, at Carrer de Sa Lluna 104.

The cafés in Plaça Constitució, Sóller, are just the place to watch the world not go by

SÓLLER
Museu Balear de Ciencias Naturales (Natural Science Museum) and Jardí Botànic (Botanical Gardens)

A manor house dating from the turn of the century is now home to Mallorca's Museum of Natural Sciences, opened in 1992. Its enthusiastic staff look after a cherished collection of fossils, animal skulls, bones, rocks and natural curiosities dating back millions of years. The surrounding grounds contain the terraced Botanical Gardens of Sóller, with plots devoted to Balearic Islands shrubs and herbal, aromatic and culinary plants. Though still evolving, both museum and gardens are worth seeking out.

Camp d'en Prohom. Signposted on the east side of the Sóller to Port de Sóller road at km30. To walk from Plaça Constitució follow signs to the Correus (post office) down Carrer de Rauza Rector, turn right into Carrer de Quadrado then right again into Carrer de Capitan Angelats. Tel: 63 40 64. Open: Tuesday to Sunday 10.30am–1.30pm and 5–8pm (3.30–5pm in winter). Closed: Monday. Admission free.

Museu de Sóller

This is in a private house on three floors packed with antiques and relics of old Sóller. In the courtyard are agricultural tools and a wine press, and upstairs religious statues and ornaments, an old-style bedroom, shell-encrusted

Crammed with exhibits, the homely Museu de Sóller evokes the past life of the town

amphorae, souvenirs of emigrants to Puerto Rico and, incongruously, masks from Papua New Guinea.
Carrer de Sa Mar 13. Open: Sunday to Friday 11am–1pm and 4–7pm. Closed: Monday. Admission charge.

35km north of Palma on the C711. Tourist Office: Plaça de Sa Constitució 1. Tel: 63 02 00.

SON MARROIG

The stately mansion that once belonged to Archduke Luis Salvador is now a shrine to Mallorca's greatest admirer. Even without its associations with this enlightened aristocrat, Son Marroig would be worth visiting simply for its millionaire setting overlooking the coastline of northwest Mallorca.

Only a part of the ground floor and one room of the first are open to the public, but you can see a wealth of *memorabilia*, including collections of

photographs, paintings owned by the Archduke and his large library. In the garden a short walk leads to a graceful Greek temple in white marble where he would sit and contemplate the sea and mountains. The rocky headland below, called Sa Foradada, is pierced by an 18m-wide hole. It is possible to walk down to the landing stage built so that the Archduke and his guests could moor their yachts and swim off the rocks. Get a ticket from the custodian in the house before you set off.
33km north of Palma, 4km west of Deià on the C710. Tel: 63 91 58. Open: Monday to Saturday 9.30am–2pm and 4.30–8pm (6pm between November and March). Sunday 9.30am–2.30pm. Closed: Sundays between April and October. Admission charge.

THE ARCHDUKE

Archduke Luis Salvador (1847–1915) was a wealthy Austrian aristocrat who first set eyes on Mallorca while yachting round the Mediterranean. An ardent naturalist, the Archduke spent a great part of his life on the island and owned several estates on the northwest coast in addition to Son Marroig. Stories of his scholastic endeavour are frequently spiced with gossip about his affair with a local girl stricken by leprosy, and every islander has an Archduke story to tell. One recalls how a farmer, unaware of who he was dealing with, gave him a few coins in reward for helping him shift some barrels. 'That is the first money I have earned in my life,' quipped the Archduke.

The rock with an eye: Sa Foradada extends into the sea below Son Marroig

A WINTER IN

Mallorca is still reeling from the visit paid to the island in 1838 by the French literary celebrity George Sand and her lover, the Polish composer Frédéric Chopin. Sand, the *nom de plume* of Baroness Amandine Aurore Lucie Dupin (1804–76), was also accompanied by her 14-year-old son Maurice and eight-year-old daughter Solange.

The Carthusian monastery at Valldemossa; portrait of Frédéric Chopin (above)

In those days there was little accommodation for foreigners available on the island. The party stayed first in a villa in Establiments,

Majorca

but were forced to move out when rumours spread among the villagers that Chopin had tuberculosis, a disease from which he eventually died in 1849. A new home was found in three cells in the former Carthusian monastery at Valldemossa, just three years after its monks had been expelled. Their stay here was far from idyllic, characterised by poor food, 'lugubrious rain', Chopin's declining health and ostracism by the locals. A free-thinking, cigarette-smoking, trouser-wearing pioneer feminist, Sand later commented how different things might have been had they bothered to attend Mass.

Mallorca has never forgiven Sand for the opinionated account of her travels given in *Un Hiver à Majorque* (*A Winter in Majorca*), published in 1842. While references to the islanders as thieves, monkeys and Polynesian savages are distasteful, her book is appreciative of the Mallorcan countryside and provides a memorable glimpse of the island just 150 years ago. Somewhat ironically, Sand's and Chopin's visit has contributed to the image of Mallorca as an island of romance and cultural pedigree, and her book is now sold in several languages in Valldemossa. The English translation by Robert Graves includes his own idiosyncratic annotations. As he observed, the whole episode was a fascinating clash of the classical and romantic worlds.

Portrait of George Sand, author of *A Winter in Majorca*, hanging in Valldemossa

Valldemossa

*T*he hillside town of Valldemossa has become associated with two women who could hardly be more different. Lording it over the defiantly pretty houses and plant-filled cobbled streets is the hulking shape of La Cartuja (Reial Cartoixa in Catalan), the Carthusian monastery where George Sand and her lover Frédéric Chopin spent the winter of 1838–9 (see pages 78–9).

Walk down the hill to the parish church though, and you will discover that Valldemossa is more concerned with remembering Mallorca's 16th-century saint, Santa Catalina Thomás. There is scarcely a house without a painted tile beside the front door asking for her support. Take Carrer de Rectoria to the left of the church to see the tiny dwelling where she was born, now restored as a shrine.

Reial Cartoixa (Royal Carthusian Monastery)

The monastery at Valldemossa developed from a royal palace given to the Carthusian order in 1399. Most of the buildings date from the 18th century when the community was at its most wealthy. Visitors enter through the gloomy neo-classical church, begun in 1751 and decorated with frescos by Bayeu, Goya's brother-in-law. You walk into huge whitewashed cloisters, where signs point out a circuit of the rooms and cells where the monks lived. Their quarters seem luxurious compared to the popular conception of monastic life, with individual prayer rooms, fireplaces and vegetable gardens overlooking the valley.

The monks prepared and dispensed medicine in the Pharmacy; after their expulsion in 1835, one remained to continue treating the villagers. Their

cells were auctioned off one by one, and some are still used as private summer residences. The head of the monastery resided in the Prior's Cell, where you can see *memorabilia* associated with Santa Catalina Thomás, the library where visitors were received, and some of the instruments of flagellation used in penitential moments.

Cells 2 and 4 recreate the rooms occupied by Sand and Chopin, and contain the manuscript of *A Winter in Majorca* and the two pianos used by the composer. A Pleyel piano sent from France took so long not going through customs that it arrived only 20 days before Chopin left. Cells 6 to 9 contain a 16th-century printing press, books and paintings belonging to the Archduke Luis Salvador and 19th- and 20th-century landscape paintings inspired by the Serra de Tramuntana. Upstairs is a museum of contemporary art with works by Miró, Picasso and Henry Moore.

Palau del Rei Sanç (King Sancho's Palace)

Next door to the monastery, this palace was originally built in 1311 as an inland hunting lodge for the asthmatic King Sancho. It was donated to the Carthusians in 1399, who lived here until 1767 when the new monastery was occupied. Today it is stuffed with a miscellany of antiques, furniture, books, utensils and religious finds, including a grim array of ever-suffering saints.

Take a wander through the well-kept narrow streets of Valldemossa, always full of plants

Open: Monday to Saturday 9.30am–1.30pm and 3–7pm (6pm between November and March). Closed: Sunday. Admission charge. Tickets for combined entry to the church, palace, monastery and museums are issued at the south side of the church. Exhibitions of folk dancing are staged on Monday and Thursday at 10.30am in the summer.

15km north of Palma, 16km southwest of Sóller. Tourist Office: Plaça de la Cartuja. Tel: 61 21 06.

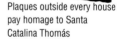

Plaques outside every house pay homage to Santa Catalina Thomás

SANTA CATALINA THOMÁS

Mallorca's own saint was born in Valldemossa in 1531. A humble peasant, Catalina spent most of her 43 years in Palma's Santa Magdalena convent, where she is buried. Her life was truly exemplary – she even mixed sand with her soup as a precaution against gluttony. Canonised in 1627, Santa Catalina is now a revered presence in many of the island's churches.

Palma to Port de Sóller

By 1917 Mallorca's railway system was at its most extensive, and you could have travelled by train from Palma to Inca, Manacor, Artà, Felanitx and Santanyí. The line to Sóller, audaciously cut through the Serra de Tramuntana, opened in 1912 and was quickly followed by a connecting tram service to Port de Sóller. An evocative survivor from a bygone Mallorca, the train with its vintage carriages is now a part of the island's tourist appeal, but the line is still used by commuters. See page 65 for route. _While the timetables allow for a shorter trip, it is best to devote a day for this journey._

This itinerary is based on weekday timetables only. If you intend to return to Palma by the last bus, tram or train of the day, check that they are running.

1 PALMA

The train leaves from the Sóller station in Plaça d'Espanya. There are five departures a day, but only the 10.40am train makes a special photo-opportunity stop during the hour-long, 27km journey. The train passes through Palma's poorer suburbs, then rattles across the tree-studded plains to the village of Bunyola. After this stop, a series of 13 tunnels are needed to get the train through the mountains. The longest, Tunel Mayor, runs for 3km.

2 MIRADOR DEL PUJOL D'EN BANYA

The purpose-built viewing stop overlooks the houses of Sóller. The

A wooden tram with orange livery has linked Sóller and Port de Sóller since 1913

Vintage trains on the Palma-Sóller railway provide a window to Mallorca's past

train pauses during playtime in the school far below, and children's cries ring around the valley.

3 SÓLLER

The 10.40am train arrives at Sóller about 11.40am. The tram to Port de Sóller leaves from just below the station, but do not join the rush to board it. Instead take a walk down the hill to enjoy the sedate delights of Sóller (see pages 75–7). There is time to visit its two museums before they close, and to have a drink or lunch in one of the the cafés in Plaça Constitució.

Return to the railway station to catch the tram, which departs on the hour and takes 30 minutes.

Some of the wooden, orange-fronted tram carriages are now over 80 years old. In the summer more modern open-sided carriages are also used. A loop in the line allows the upcoming tram to pass.

4 PORT DE SÓLLER

See page 73. Have a lazy lunch, a swim, walk round the seafront or up to the lighthouse at Punta Grossa (see page 86).

5 RETURN TO PALMA

The most scenic way to get back to Palma is by bus from Port de Sóller. Buses go at 4pm or 5.30pm from a quayside stand close to the tram terminus. The bus takes an epic route up around the coast via Deià (see page 68) and Valldemossa (see pages 80–1). The journey takes 90 minutes and terminates by Bar La Granja in Carrer de Arxiduc Lluís Salvador, which is a short walk north of Plaça d'Espanya.

If you prefer to return by train, get the 5.30pm tram from Port de Sóller and the 6.20pm train from Sóller.

Pollença • • Alcúdia
• Sóller
Palma
■
Palma Llucmajor • Manacor
Nova • Felanitx

Serra de Tramuntana

This exhilarating drive takes you from Palma up to the peaks and pines of the Serra de Tramuntana, passing the highest point of the island, Puig Major, and returning across the central plain via Inca. The round trip of 110km incorporates numerous steep roads and hairpins, and will appeal to confident drivers with a good head for heights. See page 65 for route map. *Allow 5 hours.*

Leave (or bypass) Palma by the Via Cintura ring road, taking the exit marked Sóller (C711). The city's industrial estates are soon left behind as the road makes a beeline north towards the mountains. A sharp bend heralds the start of the dizzying climb up to Coll de Sóller – on the right you pass the Moorish gardens at Alfabia (see page 64), and the excavations where a new tunnel is being built through the mountains to Sóller.

1 COLL DE SÓLLER

Port de Sóller seen from the Mirador de Ses Barques

A traditional mountain pass, Coll de Sóller (496m) offers the first of many panoramic views of the island and its peaks along this route.

Shades of green: get away from it all with a tour of the Serra de Tramuntana mountains

Descend into the Sóller Valley with its neat orchards and olive groves.

2 SÓLLER

If you intend to stop in this prosperous market town (see pages 74–7) continue through the congested inner streets to the northern outskirts, where there is a car park.

Follow the signs to Lluc, joining the C710 as it climbs east through fragrant pinewoods. A turning to the right offers a short detour to the pretty village of Fornalutx (see page 68).

3 MIRADOR DE SES BARQUES

This stunning viewpoint overlooks the Badia de Sóller, and is a convenient place to pause for refreshments. The bar-restaurant has a reputation for its freshly-squeezed orange juice, made with fruit from the prolific valleys below. From the terrace you can look down to the well-protected harbour at Port de Sóller. To the west is the Cap Gros lighthouse, and to the east the headland of Punta Grossa with the old watchtower of Torre Picada. *Continue east, climbing to a starker landscape overshadowed by craggy peaks, and Puig Major to the north.*

4 PUIG MAJOR AND GORG BLAU

Even though radar installations cap the top of Mallorca's highest peak (1,445m), and military use prevents close access by the public, Puig Major makes a formidable sight. The road skirts the mountain, burrowing through two tunnels and passing two reservoirs, Embalse de Cúber and then Embalse del Gorg Blau. The mainstay of the island's water supply, these stretches of water are surrounded by a nature reserve. The first reservoir is enlivened by a group of photo-friendly black donkeys, while Gorg Blau is a good spot for a walk or picnic.

When leaving Gorg Blau, look out for a sharp bend to the left, sometimes obscured by parked cars, which leads into a short tunnel. This is the turning down to Sa Calobra (a two-hour detour, see pages 74–5). Continue along the C710 through Escorca, reaching a junction where you turn right on to a minor road signposted to Caimari. The road makes a gentle descent through stone-walled fields to this village and Selva to reach Inca (see page 69). From here drive southwest to Binisalem and on to Palma taking the new fast motorway or the older highway via Santa Maria del Camí (see page 75).

Badia de Sóller

This walk follows the curve of the Badia de Sóller, following a narrow road that climbs up to the lighthouse overlooking the charming little fishing village of Port de Sóller. If you have taken the train and tram ride from Palma (see pages 82–3) it is a pleasant way to stretch the legs before your return journey. Keen walkers with strong footwear can continue across the cliffs, with some scrambling involved, to enjoy the views from Punta de Sóller. *Allow 90 minutes to the lighthouse and back, 3 hours if you include Punta de Sóller.*

The walk begins at the tram terminus on the seafront, next to the Restaurant Marisol.

1 PORT DE SÓLLER

Walk south along the seafront road, passing the Hotel Miramar. On the cliffs overlooking the bay you will see the white salt-cellar-shaped lighthouse you are aiming for, the Faro de Punta Grossa. Turn right by Bar Pepe, crossing the tramlines and a blue-railed bridge to follow the curve of the shore. This easy stroll provides changing perspectives of the wide, virtually enclosed bay. Though Port de Sóller is still used by fishermen and the military, new egg-box developments scaling the hillsides for a sea view are proof that it is a growing holiday resort.

2 FARO DE PUNTA GROSSA

The road now makes a steady climb that twists up the side of the cliffs, passing through pinewoods and a variety of well-

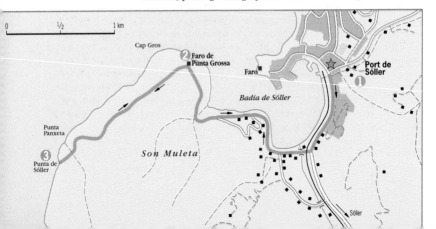

The seafront at Port de Sóller, guarded by the mountains of the Serra de Tramuntana

placed villas owned by foreign residents. From the euphorbia-covered hills, which sparkle with small yellow flowers in early spring, you can look down to the turquoise waters of the bay below. Fishing boats heading off to work or pleasure cruisers taking trippers round to Sa Calobra usually catch the eye.

In the valley below one hairpin, you can see the stony ruins of what was either a watchtower or a *forn de calç* (lime kiln), built to make the whitewash with which the islanders once painted their houses. A little further on is a memorial to a soldier killed here in the opening days of the Spanish Civil War. When you reach the lighthouse (closed to the public) there are fine views back across the port and the mountains behind, including the island's highest peak, Puig Major, with its crown of communications antennae.

3 PUNTA DE SÓLLER

To continue to Punta de Sóller, take the track to the left of the lighthouse, ducking through two chains. When the wall on your left ends, continue downhill as the path curls around the lonely cliffs. The route is well trodden but overgrown in places – look for the small piles of stones that mark the path at key points. Fragrant pines and wild rosemary enhance the journey, and you will meet more ruined lime kilns before the path descends to a river valley. Crossing a stone wall, you then scramble up the bare rocks, keeping away from the cliff-edge and passing a '67' painted on the rocks in red paint. From the summit there are rewarding views south along the coast towards Lluc-Alcari, and back to Cap Gros. To return, retrace your steps to the lighthouse and Port de Sóller.

The Northeast

*T*wo great bays fringed with fine sand and shallow water bite deep into Mallorca's northeastern corner. The resorts here are among the most relaxed on the island, and there is plenty to discover near by: the illuminated caves of Artà, the wetlands of S'Albufera, sea views from the Cap de Formentor peninsula, and the historic towns of Pollença, Alcúdia and Artà.

ALCÚDIA

Alcúdia is strategically situated at the neck of a peninsula separating the Badia de Pollença and Badia d'Alcúdia, and neatly illustrates the accreted layers of Mallorcan history. Originally a Phoenician settlement, the town was built inland from its port (today Port d'Alcúdia) as a defence against pirates and invaders. It was taken over by the Greeks, then in the 2nd century AD became *Pollentia* (meaning 'power'), the Roman capital of Balearis Major. Sacked by the Vandals in the 5th century, it was rebuilt by the Moors as

Al-Kudia (meaning 'on the hill'). With the conquest of Mallorca by Jaume I in 1229, it again came under Christian rule.

Today Alcúdia's buildings and monuments are being carefully restored. The town is boxed in by toy fort walls, and it is best to park outside these on the south side in Avinguda dels Princeps d'Espanya.

Old Town

Take the entrance to the old town next to the church of Sant Jaume, which stands at its southwestern corner. Before

THE NORTHEAST

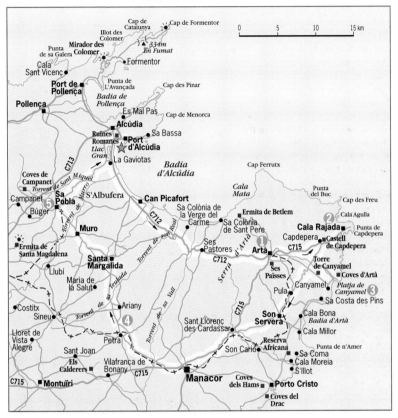

walking through, you can inspect some remnants of Roman houses lying just across the road behind a row of cypresses. The church of Sant Jaume dates from the 13th century but the present building is mostly 19th century. On Sundays it is packed with worshippers.

The Porta del Moll gate in the walled town of Alcúdia, once the island capital

To reach the town centre walk along Carrer de Sant Jaume, turning left down Carrer dels Albellons. Turn right past Alcúdia's pompous neo-classical town hall to reach Plaça Constitució. Leave by the narrow shop-lined Carrer de Moll, which brings you to the massive Porta del Moll gate. To the right is Passeig de la Mare de Déu de La Victoria, where the town's market takes place on Thursday and Sunday.

ALCÚDIA

Museu Monogràfic de Pollentia
Next to the church of Sant Jaume, this small museum is devoted to the history of Roman *Pollentia* and exhibits finds from excavations in the area.
Carrer de Sant Jaume 30. Tel: 54 64 13. Open: Tuesday and Thursday 10am–2pm. Closed: Friday to Monday and Wednesday. Admission charge.

Oratori de Sant Anna
Half a kilometre south of the town, on the road to Port d'Alcúdia, is a tiny chapel worth a visit purely for its simplicity and peaceful atmosphere. The oratory was built in the early 13th century and is believed to be Mallorca's

oldest surviving church. Above the entrance is a carved statue of the Virgin Bona Nova.
The chapel is on the north side of the road, opposite a cemetery. Open: mornings only.

Ruines Romanes
A Roman amphitheatre stands 1.5km southwest of the town, on the right-hand side of the road to Port d'Alcúdia. It has the distinction of being the smallest Roman theatre in Spain, but its tiered seats and stubby pillars have a historic aura nonetheless.
Open premises. Admission free.

Ermita de la Victoria
The peninsula northeast of Alcúdia can be visited by taking the road towards Es Mal Pas. Leave by the northern gate, Port Roja (near the bullring), and drive through the smart villas of Bonaire

The theatre at Alcúdia provides tangible evidence of the Roman presence on the island

toward Cap des Pinar. A watchtower, Torre Major, was constructed on its summit (451m) by Philip II in 1599. *En route* you will pass a turning to the right, which leads up to a fortress-like hermitage. Inside is a 15th-century wooden statue honouring Victoria, Alcúdia's patroness. Although the road to Cap des Pinar concludes in a military zone, much of this scenic headland is a nature reserve and a rewarding venue for walks, picnics or a cycle ride.
55km northeast of Palma on the C713, 11km east of Pollença.

ARTÀ

The spires and battlements of this medieval hilltop town can be seen from afar, and although Artà now has a by-pass it is well worth a visit. Known to the Moors as Jartan, Artà has an atmosphere of great antiquity that clearly emanates from its principal attraction, the Santuari de Sant Salvador. To reach this, follow signs to the centre of the town, then on and up to the sanctuary: this involves narrow streets, not always one-way. If you prefer a stiff, soul-enhancing climb, you can take the long, cypress-lined stone stairway that leads from the town centre up past the parish church of the Transfiguració del Senyor.

Santuari de Sant Salvador

The sanctuary occupies the site of a Moorish fortress. The chapel and its castellated walls were built between 1825 and 1832, the previous hermitage having been knocked down as a countermeasure against the spread of a devastating plague. The views from its courtyard over Artà's terracotta roofs and the hazy countryside beyond are engrossing – take a bag of almonds and all your unwritten postcards.

Steps leading up to the 19th-century Santuari de Sant Salvador in Artà

Open: Monday to Friday 10am–1pm and 4–7pm; Saturday and Sunday 10am–1pm. Admission free.

Museu Regional d'Artà

The museum displays archaeological finds such as ceramics, jewellery and bronzes from the nearby site of Ses Països (see page 106) and elsewhere on the island.
Carrer d'Estrella 4. Tel: 83 55 05. Open: Monday to Friday 10am–noon. Closed: Saturday and Sunday. Free.

71km northeast of Palma on the C715.

Cala Sant Vicenç, a quiet resort protected by mountains and popular with artists

CALA MILLOR

Cala Millor is the epicentre of recent tourist-wooing developments along Mallorca's east coast. From Cap des Pinar south to Sa Coma, every little bay and cove appears to have sprouted a holiday complex. **Cap des Pinar**, named after the pines growing on this headland, endeavours to remain an upmarket enclave with luxury hotels and private villas. To the south in the Badia d'Artà is **Cala Bona**. Its role as a fishing port has been superseded with the addition of three man-made beaches and it is now a good spot for watersports, with several seafood restaurants.

Cala Millor is the largest and brashest resort, with a coastline stacked with high-rise hotels and apartment blocks. Here the entertainment, like the beer, just keeps on coming – expect one long crowded party in summer. The beach has clean white sand and a wide promenade, with a good range of sports activities that include windsurfing, karting, bowling and riding. If you fancy a return to normality, walk into Son Servera for the Friday morning market.

An obstacle to the developers' projects is the protected headland at Punta de n'Amer. Just south is **Sa Coma**, another full-blown resort but quieter than Cala Millor with a great beach and tidy seafront. The roads here are reasonably flat and in good condition, making Sa Coma a good choice for an easy bike ride.

71km northeast of Palma, 15km south of

Artà. Tourist Offices in Cala Millor: Carrer de Fetjet 4. Tel: 58 58 64. Parc de la Mar 2. Tel: 58 54 09.

CALA RAJADA

Another popular holiday resort that has evolved from a quiet fishing village, Cala Rajada possesses all the seaside amenities its international clientele expect, yet still retains some native Mallorcan charm. A one-way system leads visitors to the small harbour, where there is parking and a long promenade with shops and restaurants. The beaches close to the town are nothing special, but there are appealing sandy bays further north at Cala Guya, Cala Agulla and Cala Mesquida, and at Platja Son Moll to the south.

A 2km walk uphill from the port, signposted Faro, leads through woodland to the breezy headland of Punta de Capdepera and its lighthouse.

Connoisseurs of modern art and gardens should consider visiting **Casa March**, a private estate belonging to the wealthy March family. The grounds contain sculptures by Rodin, Henry Moore, Barbara Hepworth and several Spanish artists.
Visits by appointment only through the local tourist office.

80km northeast of Palma, 3km east of Capdepera. Tourist Office: Plaça dels Pins. Tel: 56 30 33.

Sun-worship in Cala Millor

CALA SANT VICENÇ

This secluded resort is tucked away in the northeast corner of the island. Its two sandy bays, sheltered by the Serra de Cornavaques to the west and Serra de Cavall Bernat to the east, are divided by the San Pedro hotel, with a jumble of other hotels, restaurants and shops following the shoreline. Inland there are impressive villas with profusely flowering gardens. Cala Sant Vicenç, with its easygoing atmosphere and rugged cliff scenery has always been an artists' haven: a statue on its promenade pays tribute to one local painter, Llorenc Cerda Bisbal.
56km northeast of Palma, 5km northeast of Pollença.

CAN PICAFORT

In the centre of the Badia d'Alcúdia, this fishing port turned resort has a good family beach fringed with low pines. A copious supply of restaurants, supermarkets and souvenir shops meets all the needs of its visitors, who are predominantly package holidaymakers staying in the high-rise hotels. For quieter beaches head north to Platja de Muro.
64km northeast of Palma, 11km southeast of Port d'Alcúdia. Tourist Office: Plaça Igro, Carrer de Gabriel Roca 6. Tel: 85 03 10.

The Cap de Formentor peninsula offers clifftop viewpoints and inviting sands

CAP DE FORMENTOR

The peninsula of Cap de Formentor boasts some of Mallorca's most dramatic scenery, made accessible by a steep and winding road leading out to its isolated lighthouse. Leaving Port de Pollença, the road (PM221) climbs steadily with good views over the Badia de Pollença. Be sure to stop after 6km at the Mirador d'es Colomer, a breathtaking viewpoint above the sea-pounded cliffs. A small, rocky islet, Illot des Colomer, lies offshore and is a sanctuary for nesting seabirds.

From here the road narrows, with sharp bends where monster coaches love to hide. Two more small viewpoints conspire to exhaust your film stock, then the road drops down, passing a turning right for Platja de Formentor. Continue east along the spine of the peninsula for another 11km, passing through the En Fumat mountain to reach the lighthouse. This was built in 1860 and is closed to the public. Like many 'Land's Ends' around the world, Cap de Formentor can get ludicrously crowded, but few will dispute the magnificence of the sea views, which in good weather stretch to Menorca.

On the return you might stop at Platja de Formentor, a beach visited by boat excursions from Port de Pollença in the summer, or call into the Hotel Formentor for a drink (suitable dress required). Tucked into the sheltered south coast of Cap de Formentor, the hotel was built in 1926 by the wealthy Argentinian Adan Dielh and helped put Mallorca on the luxury holiday map. *84km northeast of Palma, 20km northeast of Port de Pollença.*

CAPDEPERA

At the eastern tip of the island, Capdepera and its hilltop castle can be seen from afar as you drive from Artà. The town is the centre of Mallorca's basketmaking industry and in the nearby hills you see the dwarf fan palms that provide the raw material. Try to park in the main square, Plaça de l'Orient, then walk up the steps that lead to the ruins of Castell de Capdepera. There are views back to the tightly packed roofs of the town below.

Castell de Capdepera

Constructed during the 14th century, the castle occupies a commanding site overlooking the island's east coast. You can walk round the well-preserved battlements and visit a small chapel, Nostra Senyora de la Esperança. A local legend recounts how, when the town was besieged by the Moors, the citizens of Capdepera hid within the castle walls. An image of Our Lady of Hope was placed on the battlements, and the townsfolk prayed for deliverance. At once a great fog descended, and the Moors fled. The miracle is remembered every 18 December, when Capdepera holds its Fiesta de Nostra Senyora d'Esperança.
Open access. Free.

78km east of Palma, 8km east of Artà.

COVES D'ARTÀ (Artà Caves)

Perhaps the grandest of Mallorca's subterranean wonders, these caves are signposted off the Capdepera–Son Servera road. A country lane passes the Canyamel golf course and winds alongside a high cliff to reach the entrance, a dramatic gaping hole 46m above the sea. The limestone caves were explored by Édouard Martel in 1896 and run for some 450 metres. Steep steps lead up to the entrance where guides take visitors down to the vividly illuminated halls of stalactites and stalagmites, including a 22m-high column known as 'The Queen'. At the lowest level organ music by Bach sets the scene for *The Inferno*.
82km northeast of Palma, 7km southeast of Artà. Tel: 56 32 93. Open: daily 9.30am–7pm (5pm in winter). Admission charge.

The castle at Capdepera, built in the days of piracy, originally enclosed the village

MALLORCAN MANSIONS

Luxury housing has always been a feature of the Mallorcan landscape, from the fortified *fincas* (country houses) built by Jaume I's *conquistadores* and their descendants to the aloof, security-screened villas in the hills favoured by

The main façade (top), banquet hall (left) and Mallorcan dog at Els Calderers, Sant Joan

the celebrities and *nouveaux riches* of today.

In the past the Spanish aristocracy were exempted from all taxes and property made a recession-proof investment. Many of the great palaces in Palma were built in the 17th and 18th centuries by noble dynasties. Today property and land is still passed down

the generations in Mallorca, and many families now own second homes.

Getting behind the monumental façades of Mallorca's historic mansions is a haphazard affair. Some have been turned into hotels or offices, others are open by private arrangement only, or

have closed their doors because too many visitors were attracted. In the Serra de Tramuntana, the Alfabia gardens, Son Marroig and La Granja all give clues to life in the island's stately homes.

The best place to visit, however, is Els Calderers, open to the public only since 1993. In the heart of the island, this huge 18th-century manor house, framed by level fields and farm buildings, still has an authentic, lived-in feel, as if the owners had just popped out for a minute. In the winter log fires blaze, and a black *ca de bestair*, the large smooth-coated dog native to the island, greets visitors with a wary eye. It is easy to imagine its noble residents receiving their guests, attending mass in the private chapel, sewing or listening to music – and their servants at work downstairs in the kitchen, laundry and ironing room. As the adverts put it, this really is *la otra* (the other) Mallorca. For details of access see page 98.

Rudolf Valentino's house (top); palatial courtyard in Old Palma (above); luxury by the sea (below)

The parish church at Muro, founded in the 13th century and re-built in the 16th

ELS CALDERERS

Sumptuous furnishings, family portraits and photographs, collections of fans, hunting weapons and toys in its 20 rooms help bring this noble residence to life. See also page 97.

40km east of Palma on the C715 to Manacor, near Sant Joan. Turn north at km37. Tel: 52 60 69. Open: daily 10am–5pm. Admission charge.

MONTUÏRI

Close to the Palma–Manacor road, Montuïri rests on a ridge, its old stone windmills set against the sky. The town has a church dating from the 13th century and is liveliest on Mondays when the weekly market takes place. Two kilometres to the east, a 19th-century chapel, Ermita de Sant Miquel, crowns the top of a small hill and offers panoramic views over Mallorca's central plains.

30km east of Palma on the C715.

MURO

Few tourists venture into the heart of this likeable town, which has many fine, mellow-stoned buildings. Its centrepiece is the Catalan-Gothic church, rebuilt in the 16th century, which has a colourful rose window above the west door and a 46m-long nave. In Plaça de José Antonio Primo de Rivera stand the Convent dels Mínims and church of Santa Ana. Outside the latter is a fountain and a statue of a peasant woman holding a jar of water. Fights between bulls and dogs were once staged between the ancient arcades and cloisters. Bullfights are still occasionally held in Muro's impressive Plaça de Toros, which holds 6,000 spectators. It was built in 1910 within the quarry that provided its white stone.

Museu Etnològic de Mallorca

The former town house of the Alomar family is now a museum devoted to Mallorcan traditions. There are comprehensive displays of rural furniture, local costume, agricultural tools and island crafts, including many examples of the Mallorcans' curious clay whistle known as the *siurell*.

Carrer Major 15. Tel: 71 75 40. Open: Tuesday to Friday 10am–2pm and 4–7pm. Sunday 10am–2pm. Closed: Monday. Admission charge.

42km northeast of Palma, 13km east of Inca.

PETRA

Most visitors to this remote inland town are American, for Petra is the birthplace of Junípero Serra (1713–84), founder of the Spanish Missions that grew into the State of California (see page 36). With its tall old buildings and a maze of narrow streets the town seems hardly to have changed since his day. Fortunately there are signs directing you to the sights associated with its famous son, who was beatified in 1988. At the eastern end of the town is the parish church of Sant Pere – its large stained-glass rose window is currently being restored. For an over-view of the area, visit the nearby Ermita de Bonany (see page 107).

Museu and Casa Junípero Serra

Small but well laid out, the museum brings home the epic achievements of the Franciscan friar who left the island for Mexico in 1749. Beautifully-made wooden models show the missions he founded in California, growing ever larger and more ornate over the years.

Local history: Muro's ethnological museum

Nine were established between San Diego and San Francisco in 1769–82, and another 12 after his death in Monterrey.

In the same street is the simple house where Serra was born, with a tiny loft-like bedroom and a minute garden at the rear. Across from the entrance a short lane leads to the Convent de Sant Bernadó, a mighty 17th-century church with a monument to the friar outside. Painted tiles framed with wrought iron depict the missions he founded – a gift from the people of California.

Carrer de Junípero Serra. Tel: 56 10 28. Open daily, but irregular hours. If closed follow the instructions on the door to reach the custodian at Carrer de P Miquel de Petra 2. Admission charge.

50km east of Palma, 10km northwest of Manacor.

PROBLEM IN POLLENÇA

The Badia de Pollença provides the setting for a romantic short story by the English crime writer Agatha Christie. *Problem at Pollensa Bay* was first published in 1936 as a Hercule Poirot story and chronicles the elaborate strategy with which a son breaks free from his over-protective mother to find love with a modern-thinking girl. Ending with a characteristic twist to the plot, the tale is a reminder of the pre-war world when well-spoken English holidaymakers with 'excellent hotel manners' (as Christie describes them) came to Mallorca on the steamer from Barcelona. In those days visitors would take a taxi to the new hotels around Port de Pollença, then relax with games of piquet and cocktails on the terrace.

POLLENÇA

Reached by a fast road from Palma (C713), Pollença rests in foothills at the eastern end of the Serra de Tramuntana. This attractive town is a haven of sleepy Mallorcan traditions where café life and the *siesta* roll on as if package holidaymakers had never been invented. The dignified buildings lining the dusty streets, with their ochre roofs, sun-baked walls and faded wooden shutters, could be virtually anywhere in eternal Spain – as could the street-choking traffic. Do not be deterred by Pollença's legendary parking problems. Leave your vehicle in one of the car parks on the south side of town and walk in to the central square, Plaça Major.

Pollença was put on the map by the Romans, and a Pont Romá still spans the Torrente de Sant Jordi river to the north of the town (just off the C710 to Lluc). After the Spanish conquest of 1229 Pollença came under the control of the Knights Templar, who initiated work on the parish church, Nostra Senyora dels Angels. The expulsion of the Moors and resistance against pirates is celebrated every August with a mock battle, *Los Moros y Los Cristianos,* that rages around the town during the local *fiesta.* Pollença's lively market takes place on Sunday mornings: clothes and household goods are sold near the car park, with fruit, flowers and vegetables in the Plaça Major. Local cheeses and roasted almonds are good buys.

Calvari (Calvary)

Just north of Plaça Major, the Convent de Montesió, built by the Jesuits in 1738, has been appropriated by the Ajuntament (town hall). From here, heralded by a fountain adorned with a cockerel, a flight of 365 steps, lined with cypresses that provide welcome shade in summer, leads up to a hilltop pilgrimage chapel, where the views justify the exertion (an alternative ascent can be made by car). Inside the chapel, built in 1794, is a wooden cross, allegedly dating from the 13th century, placed on the site by thankful

A proud cockerel rules over the fountain at Calvari in Pollença

Climb the steps of Pollença's Calvari for salvation and magnificent views

mariners who survived a shipwreck off Cala Sant Vicenç.

Museu de Municipal Pollença
South of Plaça Major, the 17th-century monastery of Santo Domingo has beautiful cloisters that are the principal venue for an acclaimed international music festival every summer. Inside is a small museum where winning entries from an annual international art competition are exhibited.
Claustre de Santo Domingo, Carrer Santo Domingo. Tel: 53 01 08. Open: Tuesday, Thursday and Sunday 10am–noon. Closed: Monday, Wednesday, Friday and Saturday. Admission charge.

Ermita de la Mare de Déu del Puig
Three kilometres southeast of the town (take the PM-220), a side road leads up to Puig de Maria (320m) and a small hermitage founded by nuns in the 14th century.
55km northeast of Palma, 11km west of Alcúdia.

WATCHTOWERS AND

On a map of Mallorca in 1683, displayed in the Museu Diocesà in Palma, the island is shown protected by over 40 watchtowers or fortified positions, most of them along the north coast. Watchtowers have been a feature of the Mallorcan landscape since Talaiotic times (see pages 10-11).

Watching it: Torre Paraires in Palma (left); near Estellencs (above); at Cala Pi (right)

Though normally considered as defensive look-outs, their strategic position could be used to aggressive ends too – the early Mallorcans indulged in piracy as well as suffering it.

Watchtowers still punctuate the skyline, for instance at the Mirador de Ses Animes near Banyulbufar on the northwest coast and at Punta de n'Amer on the east. More common today though, and sometimes similar in shape, are the windmills that are as

WINDMILLS

much an archetypal image of Mallorca as *ensaimadas* or the Sóller railway line. Windmills are often the first thing noticed by visitors arriving at Son Sant Joan airport, and there are more good clusters around Sa Pobla and Llucmajor.

Windmills were constructed to either grind corn or draw up water from underground. Originally they would all have had cloth sails, later replaced by wooden slats and the metal fans of today. Many have now fallen idle, but some have been converted into houses, restaurants and discothèques, or are used as unconventional advertising

hoardings and colourful declarations of patriotic and footballing allegiances. Admirers of these handsome structures, and connoisseurs of urban incongruities, might care to seek out Carrer de Industria in the west of Palma. Here, in the middle of a street lined with featureless housing, a row of five windmills stands proud, defiant sentinels from another age.

Windmills in Carrer de Industria, Palma (top) and Sa Pobla (right)

The harbour at Port de Pollença, a place for strolls and boat inspection

PORT D'ALCÚDIA

At the northern end of the Badia d'Alcúdia, Port d'Alcúdia has many functions. The harbour is home to a naval base and a busy fishing fleet, a modern marina caters to the many yachts and pleasure craft cruising the coast, and a daily car ferry service operates between here and the Menorcan port of Ciutadella. If you are interested in fishing trips, or sea excursions to Cap Pinar and Formentor, this is the place to come.

Port d'Alcúdia is a lively resort too, with a long seafront and a great variety of sports available, including water skiing, water scooters, dinghies and floodlit tennis courts. If you need to buy souvenirs or presents to take home but are not mad about shopping, Port d'Alcúdia could solve a few problems. The souvenir shops along Carrer de Vicealmirante Moreno sell anything that can be loosely described as Mallorcan.

Leather jackets, pottery, jewellery and olive wood products are worth considering. On Sunday mornings there is a market in Avinguda José Prado Suarez.

Platja de Muro

A long sweep of sand curls round from Port d'Alcúdia south to Platja de Muro, 9km northeast of Muro. The dunes here are fringed with umbrella pines and the bathing is good.

55km northeast of Palma, 3km south of Alcúdia. Tourist Office: Carrer de Pedro Mas i Reus. Tel: 54 86 15.

PORT DE POLLENÇA

Set in a splendid horseshoe bay, Port de Pollença is a comparatively quiet resort popular with British visitors. Long palm-lined promenades extend either side of the harbour – a colourful mêlée of fishing boats, yachts, and pleasure cruisers offering trips to the Formentor peninsula and Badia d'Alcúdia. Its sandy beaches are narrow and divided by breakwaters, with shallow water well suited to young children. Watersports can be found at the southern end of the bay, as well as tennis, riding and bowling. In the back streets and squares behind the seafront there is a good supply of 'pick-a-fish' restaurants and others serving *tipico* Mallorcan cuisine.

Port de Pollença has a relaxed, distinguished air with no nightclubs or blaring discos – though there is plenty of music and entertainment available in the restaurants and hotels. Here that admirable Spanish institution, the evening *paseo* (promenade), thrives – with plenty of recruits from the resort's sizeable community of foreign residents and retired visitors taking a long winter break. For disabled and elderly visitors, Port de Pollença is one of the most congenial destinations on the island.
57km northeast of Palma, 6km northeast of Pollença. Tourist Office: Carrer de Miquel Capllonch. Tel: 53 46 66.

RESERVA AFRICANA
(African Reserve)

A popular half-day family outing, this safari park is more interesting than might be expected, particularly if you arrive early when the animals are feeding. Tours can be made in your own vehicle or aboard a safari truck, following a one-way drive that takes about 45 minutes. The reserve's collection includes lions, zebras, antelope, wildebeest, ostriches and storks, and there is a Baby Zoo with young animals. Take binoculars, and double check that the windows are closed when the light-fingered monkeys spot you.
65km east of Palma, 2km west of Sa Coma on the Porto Cristo–Son Servera road. Bus: free service from the resorts of Cala Bona, Cala Millor and Sa Coma. Tel: 58 45 25. Open: daily 9am–5pm in winter; 9am–7pm in summer. Admission charge.

S'ALBUFERA, see page 138.

Are you an AA member? Ostriches regularly inspect vehicles touring the Reserva Africana

Sheep grazing beneath the trees near Sa Colònia de Sant Pere

SA COLÒNIA DE SANT PERE

At the southern end of Badia d'Alcúdia, this quiet fishing village is slowly developing into a resort. Behind it rises Puig den Ferrutx and the mountains of the Serra d'Artà, with the nearby countryside rich with vines, almond and apricot trees, and olive groves decorated with fat woolly sheep. There is a tiny harbour, a beach that is part rock, part sand, a Club Nautico, and a few shops and simple fish restaurants. With a campsite at the western end of the village, this makes a quiet base for budget travellers, with good walking around Ermita de Betlem (see page 136) and Puig de Morei.

83km east of Palma, 13km west of Artà. Take the C712 from Artà or Can Picafort and turn north (PM333-1), forking left after 5km for the village.

SES PAÏSSES

The ruins of this Bronze Age settlement, which still preserve an impressive portal and most of the perimeter walls in place, are an evocative legacy of the inhabitants of Mallorca between 1000 and 800BC. Some of the blocks used in the settlement's construction weigh up to eight tonnes. The site was probably occupied during Roman times. It is not difficult to picture the halls and dwellings, and the look-out tower that would have warned of approaching ships. Now surrounded by fields with almond and carob trees, Ses Païsses makes a pleasant picnic spot.

*68km east of Palma, 2km south of Artà.
Turn left off the C715 to Capdepera down a
signposted track. Free.*

SINEU

Sineu is the geographical bull's eye of
Mallorca. Jaume II built a royal
residence here in the 13th century, now a
convent where the nuns are still known
as *monges del palau* – the palace nuns.
Outside the massive church in Plaça de
San Marcos is a popular statue of a
winged lion, erected in honour of the
town's patron, St Mark.

On Wednesday mornings Sineu's
streets and squares are a stage for one of
the best village markets on the island –
particularly if you have urgent need of a
rabbit or some sheep. The village was
once on the railway line between Inca
and Artà, and the old station on its
eastern side has now been converted into
an art gallery, S'Estació. Sineu is also
known for its wine cellar bar-restaurants,
such as Celler Ca'n Font and Celler Es
Crup, which serve typical Mallorcan
cuisine.
*30km northeast of Palma, 12km north of
Montuïri.*

VILAFRANCA DE BONANY

Stop here to buy strings of red and green
peppers, sun-dried tomatoes, garlic,
aubergines, sweetcorn and home-grown
fruit and vegetables. Colourful local
produce hangs from many of the walls in
the village's main street, while roadside
stalls sell intriguing bite-sized doughnuts
known as *bunyelos*.

Ermita de Bonany

Crowning the Puig de Bonany (317m),
this sanctuary lies 5km southwest of

Fruit and veg at Vilafranca de Bonany

Petra. The entrance to the church is
through an imposing gate overseen by
St Paul and St Anthony with his piglet,
depicted on tiles. Inside the dark chapel
is a Bethlehem Grotto with a rural
Nativity scene, though the real attraction
of this *ermita* is the views over the central
plains from the terrace.
*Take the turning north off the C715 for
Petra, then look for a left turn down a
signposted country road that winds up the
mountain.*

*38km east of Palma on the C715 to
Manacor, 9km east of Montuïri.*

In Sineu's Plaça de San Marcos a statue of
a winged lion honours St Mark

Badia d'Alcúdia

Following the curve of the Badia d'Alcúdia, this leisurely 120km round trip runs southeast from Port d'Alcúdia to the uplands of the Serra d'Artà, then to Mallorca's easternmost promontory, Punta de Capdepera. Turning south, the drive continues inland to Manacor, then follows mainly quiet country roads back to the northeast coast. See page 89 for route. *Allow 5 hours.*

From Port d'Alcúdia take the main road south (C712), following signs to Artà. The road follows the pines and dunes of the coast with the S'Albufera nature reserve inland (see page 138). Passing the resort of Can Picafort (see page 93), the road continues east into the green hills of the Serra d'Artà.

1 ARTÀ

A medieval hilltop town dominated by the Santuari de Sant Salvador, Artà (see page 91) also has an archaeological museum with finds from the nearby site at Ses Païsses (see page 106).
Continuing east for 8km you reach the Capdepera ringroad. Follow the signs to Cala Rajada.

2 CALA RAJADA

A fishing port-cum-resort with fine beaches near by, Cala Rajada (or Platja de Canyamel, see opposite) would make a good place to stop for lunch or a swim. Follow the one-way system through the town to the harbour where you can park (see page 93).
Follow signs to the left in the direction of Canyamel and Son Servera. Turn left after 8km following signs to the Coves d'Artà (see page 95), driving past the Canyamel golf course to turn right at a junction for Platja de Canyamel.

Artichokes (left) and onions (right), born in the fields around Sa Pobla

The Santuari de Salvador in Artà, built in the early 19th century

3 PLATJA DE CANYAMEL

Recently developed as a holiday resort, Platja de Canyamel enjoys a sheltered position with a beach of fine white sand served by an arcade of shops and bars. When you leave, following signs for Son Servera, you pass the impressive fortress of Torre de Canyamel built as a look-out for pirates – now partly converted into a restaurant serving Mallorcan dishes (see page 170, under Capdepera).

After passing through the sedate old towns of Son Servera and Sant Llorenç des Cardassar, take the C715 to Manacor *(see page 122)*. *Follow the signs for Palma, but after 2km turn right for Petra.*

4 MANACOR TO SA POBLA

The road now crosses the flat and alluring landscape so characteristic of central Mallorca. Vines, aubergines, tomatoes and melons grow in the dusty soil, and the silhouettes of windmills and village churches stand out on the horizon.

By-passing Petra and Santa Margalida, follow the one-way system through Muro's maze of narrow streets *(see pages 98–9)*, *and continue to Sa Pobla.*

5 SA POBLA

Much of the land surrounding this agricultural town is reclaimed from swamps. Now known as the Huertas de la Puebla (People's Garden), the fields have rich fertile soil where strawberries, artichokes and salad crops are grown. You can park in the northeast of the town and walk back to the central square, which has some fine old houses and a 17th-century church.

Narrow twisting lanes lead past farms and an electrical power station to the main road (C712). Turn left for Port d'Alcúdia.

Bóquer Valley

This easy 6km walk starts in Port de Pollença and follows the course of the Bóquer valley down to the sea. The valley is a popular place for bird-watching, particularly in the migrating seasons (from April to May and September to October). Stout shoes, binoculars and a drink or picnic lunch are recommended accompaniments. *Allow 2½ hours return.*

From the roundabout on the seafront in Port de Pollença follow the signs to Formentor, which involves going inland and turning right by the Hotel Mar Calma. When the houses on the left-hand side peter out, turn left to pass the Oro Playa supermarket. If you are driving, park on the rough ground at the end of the tarmac road.

BÓQUER FARM

A pair of stone pillars marks the entrance to a tree-lined lane, which leads to a ridge and a large farmhouse. Do not be surprised if a chained dog serenades your arrival. As you pass, look over the stone wall to the left for a good view across gardens and orchards to the town below.
Go through a gate and uphill along a stony track to the start of the Bóquer valley.

BÓQUER VALLEY

You will soon go into a steep-sided cleft in the rocks. The track across the valley is well-worn, weaving through a sparse landscape dotted with wildflowers, small shrubs and windswept pines. Quite likely you will hear the bleating of the wild tan-coloured goats that roam the rocks above. Resident birds you might spot include black vultures, ravens and peregrines, and in spring and summer Eleanora's falcons (see box), ospreys and even a booted eagle soaring overhead. Stonechats and numerous goldfinches can be seen flitting around the grass. You may hear red-legged partridges, and

Into the Bóquer Valley: an easy walk down to the sea, popular with birdwatchers

keep an eye out for the rare rock sparrow.

After you pass through a gap in a stone wall, the sea comes into view.

CALA BÓQUER

Just offshore is the Es Colomer rock and to the left is the high ridge of the Serra del Cavall Bernat. In one place erosion has created a dramatic window in the cliffs; if you are feeling energetic, you can climb up for a closer look. The track continues down a sharp incline, passing a lazy freshwater spring that runs into a trough, to reach the small rock and shingle beach of Cala Bóquer.

When you have had a rest and enjoyed the solitude, retrace your steps to Port de Pollença. It is surprising how different the vistas seem on the way back.

ELEANORA'S FALCONS

The Bóquer valley and Formentor peninsula are an annual port of call for the rare Eleanora's falcon. This dark, long-tailed bird of prey gets its name from a 14th-century Sardinian princess who is said to have introduced legislation to protect nesting hawks and falcons. The birds often spend the winter in Madagascar, arriving in Mallorca in late April. Their nests are built among the cliffs along Mallorca's northern coast, but breeding does not take place until late summer. By September other birds are already migrating south, providing easy meat for the young falcons.

The South

*S*outhern Mallorca is predominantly flat and agricultural, a beguiling landscape of dusty towns, windmills, salt pans and relatively undeveloped beaches. In the southeast the inland plain (Es Pla) ends abruptly in the mountainous Serra de Llevant, capped with a castle and religious sanctuaries. Beyond this the island's east coast is indented with *calas* (coves), now fringed with resorts.

ALGAIDA

As its most interesting shops and restaurants are along the main Palma–Manacor road (C715) to the north, visitors usually only come across this quiet old town if they are *en route* to Puig de Randa (see page 125). Two ancient stone crosses stand at each end of the town, within which lies a muddle of narrow streets.

THE SOUTH

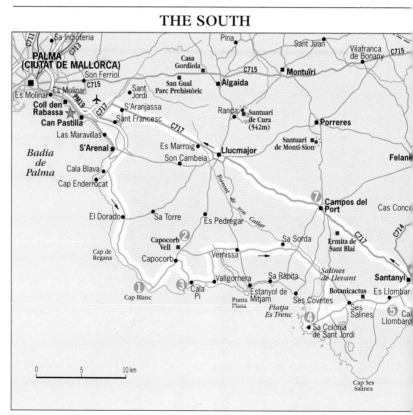

Casa Gordiola: glass (above) and the workshops that make it (top)

Casa Gordiola

Two kilometres northwest of Algaida, on the C715, stands a mock-medieval castle of circa 1969, that contains one of Mallorca's most popular tourist attractions. Here craftsmen can be seen blowing and fashioning glass, which has been made on the island by the Gordiola family since 1719. Next door to the workshop is a series of showrooms with a huge choice of glass, ceramics and souvenirs. Be sure to go upstairs to the museum, which has glass from various countries, and furniture and paintings belonging to the Gordiola family.

19km east of Palma at km19 on the road to Manacor. Tel: 66 50 46. Open: Monday to Saturday 9am–1pm (1.30pm in summer) and 3–7pm (8pm in winter); Sunday 9am–noon. Free.

Curious about cacti? Botanicactus will tell you everything you ever wanted to know

the gardens are given over to wetland plants, including a bamboo plantation and artificial lake, palms, pines, fruit trees and a Mallorcan garden. At the eastern end a nursery has tropical plants for sale.

54km southeast of Palma on the road between Ses Salines and Santanyi. The entrance is marked by a windmill with green and white sails. Tel: 64 94 94. Open: daily 9am–7pm. Admission charge.

CABRERA, see page 140.

CALA D'OR

This large, tourist-boom resort is built around a series of small bays. Its centrepiece is an Ibizan-style complex, begun in 1932, with low white buildings, spacious courtyards and an appealing range of boutiques, craft shops, bars and restaurants. The sandy beaches of Cala Gran, Cala Longa and Platja d'Or are lined with low pine trees, but can get very crowded in high season. Things have changed a bit from the conservative days when the beach at Cala Gran was reserved exclusively for men and the smaller Cala d'Or for women.

A tourist train runs from the town centre along to the marina. Packed with luxury yachts and pleasure boats this is a favourite spot for a waterfront meal. Cala d'Or is a popular venue for sporting holidays, with good facilities for sailing, diving and tennis; or you can just take a lazy boat trip along the coast to Cala Figuera.

63km southeast of Palma. Turn east at Calonge on the Santanyi–Porto Cristo road. Tourist Office: Avinguda de Cala Llonga. Tel: 65 74 63.

BOTANICACTUS

Claiming to be the largest botanical garden in Europe and still expanding, Botanicactus is a convincing desert landscape with 12,000 cacti ranging across some 400 different species. Sceptics who dismiss cacti as unchanging prickly things, fit only for cowboy films and suburban window-sills, will have to think again: the shapes, sizes and exotic blooms here are extraordinary, and include a 300-year-old Carnegie Giant from Arizona.

Stone walls have been built to protect the cacti from sea breezes, and a third of

CALA FIGUERA

Mallorca's 'Little Venice' is a narrow deepwater inlet with fishermen's houses built right up to the water's edge. If you are driving, it is best to park at the top of the port and walk down to the harbour. Here you can find idyllic postcard scenes with brightly-painted boats and villagers mending their nets or playing cards. By the time most tourist coaches arrive, the previous night's catch, unloaded at dawn and rushed away by lorry, will already be on sale in Palma's fish market. The calm waters and fjord-like scenery of Cala Figuera make it a favoured anchorage for luxury yachts. There is little accommodation and, surprisingly, only a few fish restaurants.

69km southeast of Palma, 5km from Santanyí. Tourist Office: Carrer de Bernareggi 26. Tel: 64 50 10.

CALES DE MALLORCA

Between Cala Magraner and Cala Murada, Cales de Mallorca (Coves of Mallorca) is a purpose-built, self-contained resort mixing high-rise hotels, villas and apartments with shops and restaurants. Cala Murada is relatively quiet, with a small sand and shingle beach, while Sa Romaguera is the most appealing inlet with bars and cafés close to the sea. Most nightlife is in the hotels.

Exotic-Parque Los Pajaros (Parrot Park)

The attractions of this outdoor park on the road between Porto Colom and Cales de Mallorca include displays of airborne acrobatics by parrots, a large variety of tropical birds, a cactus garden and a small zoo.

Tel: 57 33 40. Open: daily 9am–6pm. Admission charge.

73km east of Palma, 14km north of Porto

Postcard Mallorca: fishermen's houses line the waterfront at Cala Figuera

Enigmatic ruins of a settlement at Capocorb Vell, probably 3,000 years old

CAN PASTILLA

On the east side of the Badia de Palma, Can Pastilla's hotels and apartment complexes stretch inland almost as far as the airport. The resort is a mecca for fun-loving families and the young at heart looking for a beach holiday with plenty to do in the evenings. A palm-lined promenade follows the shore, particularly enjoyable at night when the lights of Palma can be seen across the water. By day the main attraction is the beach, which runs south to S'Arenal and is known as Platja de Palma. It is ideal for children, with clean white sand, shallow water, sun umbrellas, play-grounds and abundant opportunity to indulge in ice-creams.

At night Can Pastilla erupts in a blaze of neon and the ceaseless pounding of discos. The streets leading off the seafront, and along the main road leading east to Las Maravillas and S'Arenal, are crammed with souvenir shops, amusement arcades, predominantly English and German bars, and restaurants serving international cuisine.

7km south of Palma. Bus: 15 from Plaça d'Espanya.

CAPOCORB VELL

Capocorb Vell is the site of a Bronze Age settlement dating back to at least 1000BC. Concrete paths now lead among the ruins of the ancient dwellings, which still have enough of their sturdy walls, doorways, pillars, winding passages and stone floors to make a thought-provoking ghost town. Beyond the main group of buildings the remains of five *talaiots* (see pages 10–11) are spread among the fields. Near the entrance is a stone tower from where you can sometimes see the island of Cabrera.

37km southeast of Palma. Take the road from S'Arenal to Cap Blanc, or from Llucmajor towards Cala Pi, then follow signs to the site. Tel: 66 16 26. Open: Friday to Wednesday 10am–5pm. Closed: Thursday. Admission charge. Access may be difficult for disabled visitors.

CASTELL DE SANTUARI

Castell de Santuari is strategically sited at the summit of a 408m peak in the Serra de Llevant. Protected by steep cliffs, it was rebuilt in the 14th century above the ruins of a Moorish stronghold. Only parts of the outer walls and ramparts remain. Walking around the vast interior can become a scramble (unsuitable for small children), but the wildflowers and views make it well worth while.

57km southeast of Palma, 6.5km southeast of Felanitx. Take the road for Santanyí, turning left after 2km on to a country road that runs through fields and orchards then climbs up to the castle. Open: daily 10am–7pm. Admission charge.

COVES DEL DRAC

The Coves del Drac (Dragon Caves) were first explored in 1896 by a French geologist, Édouard Martel, and now attract thousands of visitors every year. The entrance to the caves is down a steep flight of steps, followed by a walk along narrow but well-lit underground passages and platforms (not for the claustrophobic).

The labyrinth of tunnels and caves is estimated to run for about 2km in total, and fanciful names have been given to many of its physical features. Visitors are guided to the delights of Diana's Bath and the Fairies' Theatre, passing through a fairyland of radiant pools and stalactites and stalagmites dramatically illuminated by concealed lights in various colours. The tour culminates in the vast Lago Martel and a cavernous auditorium that can hold over a thousand spectators. The show features a torchlight procession with musicians and singers gliding across the water in boats.

66km east of Palma, 1.5km south of Porto Cristo. Tel: 57 00 02 or 57 07 74. Open: daily with tours on the hour between 10am and 5pm during April to October; 11am–noon and 2–5pm during the rest of the year. Admission charge.

CUEVAS DEL DRACH

Come inside our Dragon Caves

CAVES

The naturally-formed caves found in Mallorca's limestone rocks have always been useful to its islanders. They provided shelter for the Pre-Talaiotic settlers who set up home here around 2000BC, and are a common thread through the island's social history. Caves provided dank homes for mythical beasts, served as refuges from slave-raiders and lairs for pirates, and were used as smugglers' dens and religious sanctuaries. Rediscovered in the late 19th century, the largest and strangest are now technicolour tourist attractions at the top of Mallorca's sightseeing charts.

Marine caves are created by the quarrying action of the waves. Inland, caves are created as water containing carbon dioxide circulates through the joints and faults in the calcareous rock. In time the passages and channels formed become caverns which are revealed when the water table drops. This process can create extraordinary deposits, including stalagmites (spikes rising from the ground), stalactites (like icicles hanging from above), draperies (like curtains) and knobbly clusters known as cave coral.

The caves at Artà (see page 95),

The gaping entrance at Artà (above); the 'Organ' inside (right)

probably the best on the island, are said to have inspired Jules Verne's book *Journey to the Centre of the Earth*, and their phantasmagoric rock shapes continue to exercise fertile imaginations. Once likened to pious subjects like the Virgin, a cathedral or grottoes fit for classical deities, these drip-fed rock blobs are now more often seen to resemble human towers, monstrous hairy nostrils, Leaning Towers of Pisa, eggs and bacon, or vegetables in a great subterranean *supermercado*.

The Inferno-like caves at Drach (above); horror movie scenery in Artà (below)

Caves (*coves*) can be visited at Drac (page 117), Hams (page 120), Artà, Campanet (page 67) and Gènova (page 50). As the temperature inside is constant all year round (about 20°C/68°F), a coat is not necessary. The ground can be wet and slippery so wear suitable shoes.

JAUME II

The present-day shape of Mallorca owes a lot to the enlightened King Jaume II, who reigned between 1291 and 1327. He established 11 new towns to encourage economic growth in the interior: Algaida, Binisalem, Selva, Sant Joan, Sa Pobla, Llucmajor, Manacor, Porreres, Campos, Felanitx and Santuari. The monarch also built new churches, bridges and reservoirs, minted a Mallorcan coinage and introduced a programme of weekly markets.

COVES DELS HAMS

The Coves dels Hams get their name from the similarity of stalactites hanging in some caves to *hams,* a Mallorcan word for fish-hooks. Though the caves are not as extensive as the nearby Coves del Drac, their underground formations, which were only discovered in 1906, are an impressive natural sight, made easily accessible by guided tour. Highlights include the 'Lake of Venice' and rock formations that resemble everything from saints and petrified cities to a herd of elephants. Coloured lights and a *concierto*

(concert) enhance the occasion.
60km east of Palma, 2km west of Porto Cristo. Tel: 82 07 53. Open: daily in summer 10.30am–1.20pm and 2.45–5.30pm; in winter 11am–1.20pm and 2.15–3.30pm. Admission charge.

ERMITA DE SANT SALVADOR

A physical and spiritual high point of the island, the Ermita de Sant Salvador is approached by a convoluted series of bends that climb up Puig de Sant Salvador (509m), the summit of the Serra de Llevant. During the ascent you pass a small chapel, the 12 Stations of the Cross, a large stone cross and a 37m-high statue of Christ the King. A well with ladle greets thirsty visitors to the monastery. Inside the huge gatehouse is a Gothic depiction of the Last Supper and offerings left by pilgrims that include pictures of local cyclists and their jerseys. The 18th-century church has a Bethlehem Grotto (a Nativity scene viewed through magnifying windows), and a revered Virgin. As photographs, crutches, toys and notes left in the small room by the entrance testify, the Ermita continues to represent a crucial source of spiritual aid. There is a simple restaurant.
57km southeast of Palma, 4km southeast of Felanitx. Take the road to Porto Colom, turning right after 2km on to a country road.

FELANITX

Felanitx is a traditional market town on the west flank of the Serra de Llevant. Its name is thought to be derived, rather poetically, from *fiel a nit* ('faithful to the night'). Seven roads converge on the

The church of Sant Miquel, Felanitx: baroque flourishes on a plain canvas

A stone cross encourages pilgrims on the winding ascent to Ermita de Sant Salvador

town, which can make parking in the narrow streets leading to its market square something of an endurance test. The square is dominated by the 13th-century church of Sant Miquel, a large, warm-stoned edifice with broad steps leading up to the Renaissance doorway. The baroque façade includes a memorial plaque to 414 victims killed when a wall in the town collapsed in 1844. Sunday morning is a good time to visit Felanitx, when the lively open-air market is in full swing and local pottery is often displayed on the church steps.

51km southeast of Palma, 13km south of Manacor.

LLUCMAJOR

Once the dominant town in the south of the island, Llucmajor is surrounded by flat agricultural land planted with dilapidated windmills. Many of the islanders in this area work in the dried fruit trade, or shoe factories.

Llucmajor is best known as the battlefield where, in 1349, the forces of Pedro IV of Aragón defeated Jaume III, so bringing an end to the short-lived independent kingdom of Mallorca. The town is liveliest on Wednesday and Sunday, when local market takes place.

25km southeast of Palma, 13km northeast of Campos.

doors, a huge domed ceiling and a slender minaret-like clock tower. Among its treasures is an image of Christ on the Cross with long straggly hair and a short white skirt.

Plaça del Rector Rubí. Open: Monday to Saturday 8.30am–12.30pm and 5–7pm; Sunday as services permit.

Pearl Factories

Artificial pearls have been made in Manacor since 1890. Today there are several factories which you can visit with an excursion or independently – follow the well-marked directions to the free parking and retail shops. The various painstaking stages in the birth of an artificial pearl can be watched from glassed-in viewing corridors. The exact recipe of ingredients is a closely-guarded

MANACOR

The largest town in Mallorca after Palma, Manacor is the centre of the island's artificial pearl industry. It has always been associated with crafts – furniture and tiles are other traditional products – and the local shopping emporia bulge with dark Mallorcan pottery, painted ceramics and items carved from olive wood. The town is also known for its local sweets, enchantingly known as *sospiros* ('sighs').

Església dels Dolors (Church of the Virgin of Sorrows)

A notable town landmark, the church of the Virgin of the Sorrows is worth the considerable effort required to track down a parking space in Manacor. Built on the site of a mosque, the church has great atmosphere, with mighty wooden

secret, but if you murmur, 'Ah yes, finely-ground fish scales mixed with resin,' it will impress your companions and not be too far off the mark. Artificial pearls are not cheap, their lustre lasts forever. See page 148 for names and addresses.
Factories generally open: Monday to Friday 9am–1pm and 3–6pm. Saturday 9am–1pm. Closed: Sunday. Admission charge.

47km east of Palma, 15km north of Felanitx.

PLATJA ES TRENC

For many visitors this is the finest beach in Mallorca. Blissfully undeveloped, with low pines, wildflowers, gently rolling dunes and a fine white sand shore that stretches for 7km, Platja Es Trenc is now a designated nature reserve. Because of its remote location it is popular with nudists. Parking can be a problem, especially during summer weekends – the recent arrival of a few sun umbrellas and a small bar are proof that, despite the beach's protected status, the tide of tourism is relentless. Most of the year the water is calm and clear, but storms can cover the beach with seaweed.

At the western end of Platja Es Trenc, close to Sa Ràpita, is Ses Covetes, a tiny village with a couple of bar-restaurants reached by driving down narrow lanes bordered by dusty fields and farmhouses with ancient windmills. Turn left when the road reaches the coast, bearing right on to a sandy track that leads to a rocky headland and white sand dunes.
56km southeast of Palma, 14km south of Campos. Take the road to Sa Colònia de

Statue of Christ in the Església dels Dolors, Manacor

A craftswoman setting pearls in gold surrounds at the Orquídea factory, Manacor

Sant Jordi then follow signs to the beach. Admission charge.

PORRERES

Embedded in the heart of the island, this quiet market town has a 17th-century church, Nostra Senyora de Consolació, decorated with painted tiles. Three kilometres southwest of the town a road climbs up to the Santuari de Montisiòn, notable for its well-preserved irregular cloisters.
37km east of Palma, 7km south of Montuïri.

PORTO COLOM

One of the many villages in the Mediterranean claiming to be the birthplace of Christopher Columbus, Porto Colom served as the port for the nearby town of Felanitx and is now a holiday resort. The tiny harbour still has its colourful old fishermen's houses and sheds, today complemented by a few souvenir shops, fish restaurants and a diving school.
63km southeast of Palma, 13km east of Felanitx.

PORTO CRISTO

Being close to the Coves del Drac and Coves dels Hams, Porto Cristo attracts coachloads of visitors who stop to enjoy its restaurants and souvenir shops. The harbour lies at the end of a long, sheltered inlet, and is still an important fishing centre. There is a small sandy beach.

Acuario de Mallorca (Mallorca Aquarium)

A 20-minute walk or short drive south of the port towards Cala Murta, and close to the Coves del Drac (see page 117), this freshwater and seawater aquarium exhibits fierce and flamboyant fish from around the world, including sharks.
Carrer de Vella. Tel: 57 02 10. Open: daily 9am–7pm. Admission charge.

63km east of Palma, 13km east of Manacor. Tourist Office: Carrer de Gual 31-A (a stiff uphill climb from the port). Tel: 82 09 31.

BREAD AND STONES

One day Jesus and the Apostles were out walking. 'Pick up a stone and follow me,' Jesus said. Seeing that they were about to climb a mountain, St Peter picked up the smallest stone he could find. When they were half-way up, Jesus stopped and blessed each of the stones they had been carrying. At once the stones turned to bread, which the Apostles ate eagerly. St Peter swallowed his measly piece in one go, but said nothing about the hunger that remained. 'Pick up another stone and follow me,' Jesus said. This time St Peter picked up a great boulder, and struggled and sweated to carry it to the top of the mountain. 'These stones will make good seats,' said Jesus. St Peter let out a silent scream, and tried to admire the view.
MALLORCAN FOLK TALE

Santuari de Cura on Puig de Randa, a Franciscan monastery founded by Ramón Llull

PORTO PETRA

Despite some stark high-rise apartments, this simple port retains its charm. Yachts and fishing-boats decorate its palm-shaded harbour and a few unpretentious restaurants serve fresh fish by their weight. Cala Montdragó to the south has a pleasant sandy beach.

69km southeast of Palma. Turn east at S'Alqueria Blanca on the Santanyi–Porto Cristo road.

PUIG DE RANDA

A striking and revered island landmark, Puig de Randa (542m) rises sharply from the agricultural plains of central Mallorca. A traditional focus for pilgrimages and religious festivals, its slopes are graced by three monasteries. To reach them drive through the village of Randa, passing the Celler de Randa bar-restaurant, and follow the signs up to Santuari de Cura (PM501-8).

The road climbs through a series of hairpins to reach a gateway to the right, where a driveway leads to the 15th-century church and medieval hostelry of

Santuari de Gràcia. From here there are fine views over the south of the island. A short drive further uphill, on the right, comes the **Santuari de Sant Honorat**, a 14th-century hermitage with venerable trees in its courtyard. To the left of the monastery a passage leading to the church is lined with painted tiles recalling the sanctuary's history.

Santuari de Cura

Continue corkscrewing up to the summit of Puig de Randa. Despite the competing presence of a radio mast, the sacred aura of Santuari de Cura lives on – not least because of the magical views its terraces offer over much of the island. Founded by the theologian Ramón Llull in the 13th century, the monastery has a gracious and cool courtyard and an ancient library with some of Llull's prayerbooks and manuscripts (ask for admission if it is not open). In the church stained-glass windows tell the story of the founder's life (see page 36).

26km east of Palma, 5km south of Algaida. Turn east off the Algaida–Llucmajor road for Randa village.

Monster fish at Porto Cristo's Aquarium

Having a splashing time at Aquacity, a fun-for-all water park in S'Arenal

attractions are landscaped swimming pools, kamikaze water slides, a Hawaiian wave pool, a mini zoo and farm, parrot show, shops, restaurants – even an antique typewriter museum.

At the southern end of the motorway from Palma, take Salida 5 signposted to S'Arenal and Cap Blanc. Bus: L23 Aquacity special goes from Plaça d'Espanya. Tel: 49 07 04. Open: May to October 10am–5.30pm. Closed: Saturday. Admission charge plus extra fees for some attractions.

11km south of Palma. Bus 15 from Plaça d'Espanya.

S'ARENAL

This pulsating tourist mecca has a long, white sand beach that attracts both foreign holidaymakers and locals escaping the urban jungle of Palma. A continuous line of high-rise hotels and apartment complexes follows the shoreline, fronted by a long promenade (recently rebuilt) that hosts an endless and infinitely watchable parade of vendors and fun-in-the-sun addicts. The beach here is often packed, which is how everyone likes it, and there are *balnearios* (bathing stations) and playgrounds for the children. In the summer a tourist train runs along the 7km seafront between S'Arenal and Can Pastilla to the north. At night this strip turns to neon and noise as bars, restaurants, discos and strip joints compete for the holidaymaker's custom.

Aquacity

Advertising itself as the world's largest water funfair, Aquacity makes exuberant efforts to keep everyone in the family happy. Among its many thrills and

SA COLÒNIA DE SANT JORDI

This is one of Mallorca's quieter seaside resorts, with sprawling modern buildings that rather mar the charms of its small harbour, Port de Campos. Once the haunt of smugglers from the North African coast, its waters are now popular with pleasure boats and glass-bottomed vessels offering excursions around the coast and south to Cabrera.

52km southeast of Palma, 15km south of Campos. Tourist Office: Carrer de Doctor Barraquer 5. Tel: 65 54 37.

SANTANYÍ

Santanyí is famous for being the source of the warm-toned sandstone that adorns many of the island's important edifices, including Palma's cathedral and Castell de Bellver. A gateway in Plaça Port is a reminder that the town was enclosed by fortified walls in medieval times. The dominant sight, though, is the church of Sant Andreu which has an enormous rococo organ rescued from the Dominican convent in Palma.

Santuari de Consolació

Five kilometres northeast of the town a
country road leads left, passing a quarry,
to wind up to the little-visited Santuari
de Consolació. Here a 16th-century
hilltop chapel houses a gentle-faced
Madonna, and there are extensive views
of the surrounding countryside. Subtract
the modern eyesores along the coast, and
it is not hard to imagine the days when
devout pilgrims climbed up the stone
steps in search of tranquillity and
consolation.

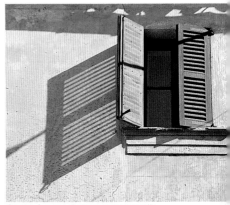

Santanyí: green shutters on warm walls

Cala Santanyí

This wide sandy cove lies 7km to the
south off the road to Cala Figuera (see
page 115). There is a beach bar and
amusements, and to the south Es Pontas,
a dramatically eroded rock bridge close
to the cliffs.

55km southeast of Palma on the C717.

SON GUAL PARC PREHISTÒRIC
(Prehistoric Park)

Drivers on the Palma–Manacor road
beware! Replica prehistoric monsters
have been spotted lurking in the scrubby
woodland west of Casa Gordiola, part
of a 30-strong collection of actual-size
models of the weird and wonderful
creatures that once lumbered round the
planet. Somehow they all ended up in
this fun-for-all theme park.
*21km east of Palma, 9km north of
Llucmajor. Tel: 66 31 71. Open: daily
10am–8pm. Admission charge.*

Es Pontas, a natural rock bridge near the
relaxed cove of Cala Santanyí

The Tranquil South

This circular tour of 123km leaves the frenzy of the Badia de Palma for an easygoing drive around the cliffs, coves and sandy beaches of Mallorca's southern coast. The route then heads inland, returning through a fertile countryside of farms, windmills and historic towns. See pages 112–113 for route map. *Allow 5 hours.*

Start from Can Pastilla, taking the coastal dual carriageway east. Drive through S'Arenal and uphill to a roundabout. Turn right following signs to Cap Blanc, passing Aquacity (see page 126) on the left and Cala Blava to the right. Follow the coast south to Cap Blanc.

1 CAP BLANC

A remote, rocky headland punctuated by a lighthouse, Cap Blanc offers clifftop walks and sea views across to the island of Cabrera.
Continue northeast for 5km to Capocorb Vell.

2 CAPOCORB VELL

This is one of the most important prehistoric sites in Mallorca, with five *talaiots* and Bronze Age dwellings dating from around 1000BC (see page 116).
Drive south for 4km to reach Cala Pi.

3 CALA PI

Once an island secret, this tiny *cala* lies tucked away beneath thick pinewoods. Developers are now building luxury villas and apartments around the inlet, but you can still enjoy the clear turquoise waters and sandy beach, reached by climbing down steep steps. Beside the restored watchtower is a viewpoint with

The restored 16th-century town hall in Campos, the epitome of rural insularity

parking and a bar-restaurant.
Follow the signs for Vallgornera, then drive inland and turn right in the direction of Campos and Sa Colònia de Sant Jordi.

4 SA COLÒNIA DE SANT JORDI
Along the way rural roads lead south to the small resorts of S'Estanyol and Sa Ràpita, and the splendid beaches at Ses Covetes and and Platja Es Trenc (see page 123). After 14km turn right, passing salt lakes, the Salines de Llevant, on the right, to reach the resort of Sa Colònia de Sant Jordi. A range of bars and restaurants make this a convenient place to stop for a drink or lunch (see page 126).
Continue east towards Santanyí. 3km outside the town turn right, passing through low pines to reach Cala Llombards. A steep road leads down to the Platja (beach).

5 CALA LLOMBARDS
The sandy beach in this small resort is sheltered by wooded cliffs and has shallow waters suitable for young children. A short rocky walk by the sea provides a good view over the cove.
Return to the main road and turn right for Santanyí.

6 SANTANYÍ
This old Mallorcan town, like Campos further on, is a world away from the island's brash tourist resorts. Sturdy buildings line its narrow streets, constructed with the local honey-coloured stone that graces many of Mallorca's great buildings (see pages 126–7).
Take the C717 west to Campos.

Clear waters at Cala Pí – no longer an undiscovered cove, but still most acceptable

7 CAMPOS DEL PORT
Founded by the Romans, Campos has a mighty 16th-century church which boasts a work attributed to Murillo, *El Santo Cristo de la Paciencia* (*The Christ of Patience*), which hangs to the right of the altar. Across the road the recently restored Ajuntament (town hall), with its balustrades and coat of arms, is a monument to the civic pride of this sleepy agricultural town.
Follow the fast C717 through Llucmajor to Can Pastilla and Palma.

Mother and child in Campos

Serra de Llevant

This comfortable 4km walk, which includes a fairly stiff climb at the end, takes you to the summit of the Serra de Llevant, the ridge of hills that cuts across the southeast of the island. It begins just below the historic Castell de Santuari (see page 117) and ascends to the Ermita (Santuari) de Sant Salvador (510m). A car can be parked at either end, and the walk is equally enjoyable if done in reverse. Sturdy shoes are required. *Allow 90 minutes one way.*

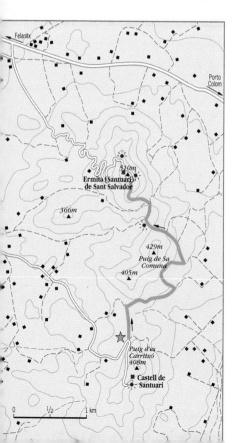

To reach the start of the walk, take the road south from Felanitx towards Santanyí. Turn left after about 2km on to a country lane signposted to Castell de Santuari. Continue until the road starts to climb in a sharp bend to the right. At the next bend park on the rough ground to the left, where a track leads east from the road.

VALLEYS AND ORCHARDS

The first part of the walk, which is variously marked by yellow and red paint marks on the trees and stones, follows a gently undulating route along a valley and through a mixed orchard. *After about 50m turn left along a narrower path, crossing a boundary wall where the ground begins to rise. Joining a forest track, continue to an orchard with carob, almond and fig trees. Turn left to walk through this to a gateway (marked with paint) near a farmhouse. Go straight across the next field.*

PUIG DE SA COMUNA

Enjoy the rural views and the many wild shrubs and flowers, such as French lavender, rosemary, heather and the colourful strawberry tree (*Arbutus unedo*). The route crosses several other tracks, then skirts eastward round a hill, Puig de Sa Comuna. As you start to

The Ermita de Sant Salvador was built on the summit of the Serra de Llevant

climb, a huge stone statue of Christ will soon come into view.
Continue up a narrow track, which rises to a small ridge.

ERMITA (SANTUARI) DE SANT SALVADOR

From here you can see the great buildings of the Ermita de Sant Salvador. The route now follows a well-worn path that rises steeply. The effort of the climb will be admirably rewarded by the splendid view from the *ermita,* where water, food and an antiquated toilet await the walker. Founded in the 14th century, this magnificent sanctuary has become a magnet for both tourists and religious pilgrims (see page 120).
Retrace your steps to return to your starting point.

TREES OF GOLD
The carob tree (*Ceratonia siliqua*), sometimes known as the locust tree, thrives in the hot arid soil of the Mediterranean region. The tree has thick shiny leaves, a gnarled trunk and long seedpods that turn from green to black as they ripen. High in sugar, these are primarily used as animal feed. The fruit of the carob is also made into a chocolate substitute sold in health food stores. The word 'carat', used today as a unit of weight for gold and precious stones, derives from the word carob. The Arabs knew the fruit as *kirat,* and the Greeks as *keration.*

Wildlife

*T*he star character of Mallorcan wildlife has long been extinct. Six million years ago *Myotragus* stalked the Balearic Islands, a peculiarly-shaped antelope with eyes at the front of its head and buck teeth that functioned like a pickaxe. By comparison the creatures currently scurrying around Mallorca appear unexciting: four types of snake (all non-poisonous), a rarely seen spotted civet cat, goats, hares and rabbits, frogs, toads and various insects. Only on the island of Cabrera, a protected wilderness, do a few endemic species of lizard arouse the visitor's curiosity.

Look skyward though, and it's a different picture. Mallorca is of great interest to ornithologists and birdwatchers, and flocks of binocular-addicts regularly descend on the island in April and May for the migration season. Hoopoes, Eleanora's falcons (see page 111), black vultures, red kites and several types of eagle cause particular excitement. Diverse habitats that include wetlands, saltpans, rocky cliffs and offshore islets – as well as the woods and forests of Mallorca's mountains – enhance the appeal of the island to both birds and their admirers.

Hunting remains popular with a powerful section of the community: wild goats, rabbits, quail, turtle doves, wood pigeon, partridges, mallards and coots are some of the targets. The wholesale slaughter of migrating thrushes is also permitted using purpose-made nets known as *filats de coll*. The farmers consider the olive-loving birds a pest, while cooks see them as a country delicacy. Restrictions were recently introduced to promote more responsible hunting – the fine for killing a black vulture, once in danger of extinction here, is now half a million pesetas.

As in so many parts of the Mediterranean, wildlife and the natural landscape are under threat from development. Fortunately, through the efforts of the environmental group GOB (Grupo Ornithologia Balear) and the local authorities, almost a third of the island is now protected in some way.

Birds: bee-eater (left) hoopoe (above);

GETTING AWAY FROM IT ALL

'Sun, sea, mountains,
spring water, shady trees,
no politics.'
ROBERT GRAVES
1965

Getting Away From it All

*T*he clichéd view of Mallorca as two islands, one passionately devoted to summer holiday fun and another real, rural and eternal, is perfectly true. Wherever you stay, all parts of the island are accessible in a day trip, and no visit to Mallorca will be complete until you have sneaked off to at least one of its quieter corners.

BOAT TRIPS

Taking to the seas is a good way to escape the crowds and see Mallorca from a different viewpoint. Glass-bottomed boats provide an opportunity to observe the marine life underwater, and some trips call into beaches, coves and sea-caves that would otherwise be impossible to reach – notably the 100m-long Cova Blava (Blue Cave) on the island of Cabrera, where the reflections of the light create an intense blue.

Except in the Badia de Palma, excursions only run in the summer (May to October in many cases) and often take the best part of a day – check if you need to bring a packed lunch, and put on plenty of suntan cream. Tourist offices have a detailed leaflet of excursion times and prices, but the following are the main links. (Signs saying *alrededores* mean a short trip in the waters close to your departure point.)

Palma and west of Palma

Trips around Badia de Palma and west to Magaluf, Portals Vells and Sant Telm. Boats leave from the jetty opposite Auditòrium on the Passeig de Marítim. *Tel: 24 20 06.*
S'Arenal west to Badia de Palma and Marineland. *Tel: 26 30 27.*
Peguera west to Sant Telm and Sa Dragonera. *Tel: 68 64 99.*
Port d'Andratx to Sant Telm. *Tel: 24 66 98.*

Boat trippers leaving Port de Pollença

On your bike: cyclists coasting along the level seafront at Port de Pollença

North coast
Port de Sóller west to Cala Deià, Na Foradada, Port de Valldemossa and Sant Telm; east to Sa Costera, Cala Tuent and Sa Calobra. *Tel: 63 01 70.*
Port de Pollença to Cap de Formentor. *Tel: 86 40 14.*
Port d'Alcúdia north to Cap des Pinar and Formentor; and Can Picafort north to Cap de Menorca and Cap des Pinar. *Tel: 54 48 11.*

East coast
Cala Millor north to Cala Bona, Canyamel and Cala Rajada; and south to Porto Cristo and Cala Barques.
Tel: 82 24 80.
Cala d'Or to Cala Figuera.
Tel: 65 70 12.

CYCLING
Cycling in Mallorca is a growth industry. The Spanish take it very seriously, and every Sunday the hills appear alive with luridly coloured insects covering great distances and heights with astonishing ease.

It is usually too hot in July and August to enjoy a major expedition, but you can have a good time just hiring a bike in a resort for a day and pottering along the coast. Some hotels have bicycles for rent or there are specialist shops. Family bicycles with seats for two adults and four children are sometimes available. You may be asked for a deposit. In Palma bicycles can be hired from Ciclos Bimont, Plaça del Progres 19. *Tel: 45 05 05.*

The Badia d'Alcúdia is obligingly flat, and a cycle path runs between Port d'Alcúdia and Can Picafort. You can cycle in the S'Albufera nature reserve too. Another *pista de bicicletas* (cycle track) curls round the centre of the Badia de Palma from Portixol west to Sa Pedrera, passing right along Palma's seafront; Castell de Bellver makes a rewarding goal. Plans are currently afoot to turn the old railway track from Inca to Artà into a green trail for walkers, riders and cyclists.

If you prefer more of a challenge, ask for the *Guia del Ciclista* map available from tourist offices. This details six itineraries ranging from 70km to 150km, including a masochistic 14km ascent from Sa Calobra.

HIDDEN CORNERS

There is nowhere on Mallorca that is 'undiscovered' but it is not hard to find somewhere that feels well away from it all. The following destinations all offer a degree of escape.

Cap Blanc

A breezy headland at the southwest corner of th island with white cliffs dropping sheer to the sea 60m below. The cliff-edges are unguarded but you can follow an invigorating walk that leads west from the lighthouse.

Cala Mesquida

In the northeast corner of the island, a once secluded beach reached by a 8km road north from Capdepera. Though busy in summer, it can be pleasantly quiet out of season.

Cala Sant Vicenç, see page 93.

Castell d'Alaró, see page 66.

Carboneros (charcoal burners) site

Cap de Ses Salines

The flat, southern tip of the island offering views across the sea to Cabrera. Military land restricts walking.

CHARCOAL BURNERS

Among the ancient mule tracks and goat-trodden paths that criss-cross the Mallorcan countryside are routes forged by the island's *carboneros* (charcoal burners). Until the arrival of the gas bottle in the 1920s, most cooking on Mallorca was done with charcoal. The burners and their families would move into the forests for the summer, building temporary homes and circular mounds of stones where the charcoal was made. Vast quantities of wood needed to be gathered using only axes and saws, and the fires had to be constantly tended. Walkers will encounter abandoned moss-covered *sitjas* (charcoal ovens) – forlorn monuments to an arduous trade.

Ermita de Betlem

A remote mountain sanctuary (380m)
reached by a tortuous road that winds
for 10km northwest of Artà. Founded in
1805, Ermita de Betlem is still home to
hermits, who no doubt find spiritual
succour in the stupendous views.

Galilea, see page 52.

Orient, see page 72–3.

Puigpunyent, see page 58.

Punta de n'Amer

A respite from the resorts on the east
coast, Punta de n'Amer can be reached
by walking north from Sa Coma or
south from Cala Millor. The 17th-
century Castell de n'Amer, with a deep
moat and ramparts offering fine coastal
views, is the high point of this 200-
hectare protected headland. It was here
that Republican forces from Menorca
landed during the Spanish Civil War.

LA RESERVA

On the eastern slopes of Puig de Galatzó
(1,026m), this privately owned nature
reserve provides a trouble-free
introduction to the countryside of
Mallorca's Serra de Tramuntana. A
network of purpose-built paths and steps
leads visitors through a 20,000-hectare
park with dense woods, 30 waterfalls,
springs, caves and rocky limestone
outcrops. Wooden plaques provide
information along the way about La
Reserva's numerous plants – most grow
naturally, with others introduced from
around the island.

Only recently completed, La Reserva
took seven years of preparation – and it
shows. Handrails are provided beside
steep steps, there are plenty of

strategically placed
benches for a rest, and information
boards in several languages provide
background on subjects like unusual
rock formations and birdlife. Additional
points of interest are a charcoal burner's
hut, a thousand-year-old olive tree and
the Cova des Moro (Cave of the Moor,
Point 9).

The walk takes 90 minutes. If you
are coming by car, try not to arrive too
late, so as to avoid driving back down
the mountains in the dark. On Fridays
in the summer the park can be visited by
coach excursion from Santa Ponça and
Peguera.

*18km west of Palma, 4km west of
Puigpunyent, signposted on the
Puigpunyent–Galilea road. Tel: 61 66 22.
Open: Wednesday to Sunday 10am till
sunset (last ticket sold 2 hours before).
Closed: Monday and Tuesday. Admission
charge.*

Another Mallorca: the S'Albufera wetlands are an unexpected treat for nature-lovers

In the 18th and 19th centuries outbreaks of malaria prompted ambitious schemes to drain S'Albufera, and from early in this century until the 1960s it was used to grow rice. Then its northern end was sold off for tourist developments. Fortunately, in 1985 800 hectares were bought by the Balearic Islands government for conservation.

Pay a visit to the Parc Naturel de S'Albufera today and you will encounter a wholly unexpected aspect of Mallorca. Marked paths, some of which can be cycled, guide visitors around the level marshland, a hushed world of bridges, hides and observation points tucked away among the lakes, reed beds and grassy undergrowth. Birds are the main attraction – over 200 species have so far been recorded, including ospreys, falcons and numerous marsh birds. Purple herons, spotted crakes, plovers, grebes, warblers, nightingales and the rare long-eared owl have all been found breeding here. Frogs, snakes, insects and colourful wildflowers like the grape hyacinth and elegant orchids add to the natural show.

5km south of Port d'Alcúdia. Turn west by the Pont dels Anglesos on the Alcúdia–Artà road. Tel: 89 21 59. Open: daily 9am–7pm (5pm November to March). Free.

S'ALBUFERA

Early maps of Mallorca clearly show how the wetlands at S'Albufera were once a lagoon – their name derives from the Arabic *Al-Buhayra*, meaning 'small lake'. The history of this extraordinary area dates back to Roman times: Pliny writes of purple herons and night herons being sent from the Balearic Islands to Rome as gastronomic delicacies, and they probably came from here. In later centuries the marshes were used as hunting grounds, and in the 17th century divided into self-irrigating cultivable plots.

SA DRAGONERA

The dramatic island of Sa Dragonera lies close to Mallorca's western tip and provides a spectacular focus for boat excursions from Sant Telm and Port d'Andratx. A steep, bare wedge of rock rising to 310m, it was famously occupied in 1977 by environmentalists protesting against the seemingly unstoppable sacrifice of the Mallorcan coast to the great god Turismo. Today what might have been an exclusive 750-building holiday resort is a protected area, and although you are not allowed ashore, many visitors like to tour Sa Dragonera's shores in the hope of spotting Eleanora's falcons, gulls and other birds of interest.

For boat excursions see page 134–5.

WALKING

With its absorbing variety of mountain, coast and plain, along with countless sanctuaries, watchtowers and castles to provide rewarding goals, Mallorca is ideal for walkers. Good launch pads, with generally quiet accommodation, are Banyalbufar, Port d'Andratx, Port de Sóller and Port de Pollença. There is a good case for staying in or near

Palma, as it is the focal point for all bus routes and offers a stimulating contrast to the rural scene.

Several specialist books on walking in Mallorca are available. Try to buy them before you leave home. Some local tourist offices, notably those in the Calvià area, produce free booklets with suggested routes. The best source of up-to-date information and advice, though, is always your fellow walkers.

The Serra de Tramuntana, with its cool forests and wide-ranging views, is the most appealing area for walking. The island's good bus service means that in many cases you do not need to hire a car – Sóller and Lluc are popular starting points. Caution is always required: beware the fierce heat and sun in summer, and mists and wet ground at other times of the year.

The steep-sided island of Sa Dragonera can be toured by boat from Sant Telm

Cabrera

*T*he island of Cabrera (Goat Island) lies 18km off Mallorca's south coast and is the largest in a scattering of islets. Roughly 7km by 5km, its coastline is indented and craggy and rises no higher than Na Picamosques (171m), the 'Fly Bite'. In 1991 Cabrera became a protected Parque Nacional Marítimo Terrestre (National Land-Sea Park), the first of its kind in Spain and a triumph of ecological lobbying.

Today the island is virtually uninhabited, but its rocks are forever stained by a grim episode during the Peninsular War when 9,000 French prisoners of war were dumped on Cabrera following the Spanish victory at Bailén in 1808. Left with only meagre water and rations, the defeated soldiers fell victim to disease, indiscipline and chronic thirst. By 1814, when the survivors were finally taken off, over 5,000 prisoners had died. A monument near the small port remembers the victims of this tragedy.

In 1916 Cabrera was taken over for military use, and a handful of soldiers are still stationed on the island – today joined by visiting scientists, naturalists and day trippers from the mainland. Cabrera has a superb natural harbour, and the island was often used as a stepping-stone for pirates raiding the Balearic Islands. The shell of a 14th-century castle-cum-prison still stands on a nearby hilltop, but is officially out of bounds.

The appeal of Cabrera today is its rarity: a wilderness island in the midst of the over-developed Mediterranean. Among the many birds attracted here are Eleanora's falcons, cormorants and a colony of rare Audouin's gulls. Wild goats, an exclusive sub-species of Lilford's wall lizard, and a rich marine life all thrive here.

Boat excursions to Cabrera depart from the port at Sa Colònia de Sant Jordi daily between May and mid-October.

Tel: 64 90 34. The trip takes a full day – take a picnic, swimming costume and snorkel. Information on the island is available from the Sa Colònia de Sant Jordi tourist office, see page 126.

Feral goat (left) and Audouin's gull (below)

DIRECTORY

'*The first difficulty that a stranger encounters on a shopping expedition in a Majorcan village is the absence not only of shop signs but of shop fronts. Everybody knows where the shopkeeper lives, so why should he announce it?*'

GORDON WEST
Jogging Round Mallorca 1929

Shopping

*P*alma is the place to shop in Mallorca. Specialist factories making glass, artificial pearls, leather goods and carved olive-wood items are also worth visiting – their wares are not necessarily cheaper than in normal shops, but it is always fun to know the provenance of your purchases.

OPENING TIMES

Shops generally open up between 9am and 10am depending on what they deal in – those selling fresh produce open earliest. By 1.30pm they are closing down for lunch. They re-open around 4.30 to 5.30pm, then remain open until 8pm. Shops tend to have longer opening hours in the summer, and in the resorts some stay open through the lunch break, as do hypermarkets. On Saturday shops open in the morning only. For the truly indefatigable shopper, there is a department store in Palma, the Galerias Preciados in Avinguda Jaume III, that is open Monday to Saturday 10am–9pm. English is spoken in many shops.

Spain is a procrastinator's paradise, and the spirit of *mañana* ('why do today what can be put off till tomorrow?') thrives in a happy-go-lucky island like Mallorca. In some country shops it can take so long to be served it might be necessary to check the sell-by date on your purchases. Dare to look impatient, and you will be dismissed as an imbecile from the rat race.

Have a hat: shopping in Mallorca is a relaxed affair, but there are few bargains

Palma has the best choice of shops, with a web of traffic-free streets to explore

beachwear are worth considering. A comprehensive range of Spanish and Mallorcan souvenirs can be found at the Poble Espanyol complex in Palma (see page 41). Local craftmaking skills are also displayed here.

SUPERMARKETS

All the resorts have well-stocked supermarkets. Years of experience have taught owners about the money to be made from selling tomato ketchup, Heinz beans and Marmite, and there is little need to take such staples out to Mallorca. Imported goods tend to cost more than Spanish brands. Vegetables are sold by the kilo, and at fish, meat or delicatessen counters remember that you usually have to take a numbered ticket from a machine to be served in turn.

If you are staying in a self-catering apartment or inland villa, it may help to load up your rented car at one of the hypermarkets on the outskirts of Palma. You will need a 100 *peseta* coin to get a trolley, and in some premises personal bags must be left at a counter. Hyper-markets are generally open 10am–10pm Monday to Saturday only (see pages 147 and 148 for addresses).

PRICES

Shoes, T-shirts and casual clothing are good value, and '100 *Peseta*' shops, where all goods are theoretically that price or less, is a purse-friendly way to indulge the kids. Many shops appear to be in a permanent state of sale (*rebaja*). Sizes of clothes and shoes will be in metric and European sizes (see page 180 for conversion tables). Bartering is rarely necessary, though the itinerant market vendors from West Africa found in markets and seafront pitches will oblige. It is a common diversion at Palma's Rastrillo flea market.

SOUVENIRS

The range of items for sale bearing the word 'Mallorca' or a relevant image is a tribute to the ingenuity of the islanders. While some goods are mesmerisingly unnecessary to world progress, glass, kitchen pottery, olive-wood utensils, candlesticks, tableware, tea-cloths and

Many Mallorcan souvenirs are hand-made

ISLAND CRAFTS

It is ironic that the best souvenirs Mallorca produces are also the most breakable. Among the glut of holiday merchandise on sale around the island, the brittle, curiosity-provoking *siurell* is the one craft product that feels truly Mallorcan. Made from clay and often painted white with flashes of red and green, these ancient tokens of friendship usually take the shape of a behatted figure on a donkey or playing a guitar. They come in varying sizes and incorporate a crude whistle at the base. The origin of the *siurell* is uncertain. They are known to have existed in Moorish times but probably date from much earlier. The artist Joan Miró was fond of these naïve works, which are mostly made around Marratxí.

Glass is another exceptional product and has been made on the island since Roman times. In the 16th century Mallorcan glassware rivalled that of Venice, and today's bestselling products often reproduce historic designs. Since the 1960s the island has had three glassmaking centres – the best known is Casa Gordiola at Algaida. Here visitors can see craftsmen hand-blowing the glass, which is made in dark green, cobalt and amber hues. Jugs, drinking glasses, vases and candle-holders are popular buys.

A robust semi-glazed brown pottery is made in Felanitx, and the Sunday morning market here is a good place to pick up cooking bowls or jugs. Local olive wood is carved into domestic utensils and ornaments at the Oliv-Art factory near Manacor; the mellow-grained wood is hard-wearing and makes worthwhile presents. *Roba de llengues*, literally cloth of

Look out for clay figures known as *siurells* (left), ceramics (below) and carved olive-wood (far right)

Pottery student at Poble Espanyol, Palma (left);
painted plates for decoration or dining (below)

tongues, are a striking feature of the
Mallorcan home. Made mainly in
Pollença, this durable and reversible
cotton material often comes in
zigzagging red, green or blue patterns
and is used for curtains, bedspreads,
wall furnishings and upholstery.

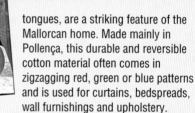

Shopping in Palma

*A*ll the useful shops are within the boundary of the city's old walls. Most of them are on the east side of Passeig des Born where many streets are traffic-free. Whether you actually have things to buy, or just enjoy the bustle of a city at play, the streets and squares listed below are all worth getting to know. Early evening, when the Palmese indulge in window-shopping, cake-buying and the how-do-you-do traditions of the Spanish *paseo* (promenade), is the most enjoyable time for exploration.

Avinguda de Jaume III: Palma's quality shopping street.

Carrer de Sindicat: bargain clothes, shoes, spices.

Carrer de Sant Miquel: links Plaça Major and the market.

Carrer de Plateria: jewellery shops galore.

Carrer de Jaume II: fans, umbrellas, boutiques.

Plaça Major: enclosed square with many shops down below.

La Rambla: flower stalls and newspaper kiosks.

ANTIQUES
Linares
Close to the cathedral.
Plaça Almoina 4. Tel: 71 72 19.
Persepolis
High-class antiques in main shopping street.
Avinguda de Jaume III. Tel: 72 45 39.

ARMY SURPLUS
B52
Military *memorabilia*, mugs, badges, uniforms.
Carrer de Brossa 14. Tel: 72 44 24.

BOOKS
Anticuari Ripoll
Old prints and books.
Carrer de Sant Miquel 12. Tel: 71 74 36.

CAKES AND CHOCOLATES
Frasquet
Chocolates and sweets for all moods.
Carrer de Brossa 19. Tel: 72 13 54.
Forn d'es Teatre
Most photographed cake shop in Palma.
Plaça Weyler 11. Tel 71 52 54.
Forn Fondo
The place for *ensaimadas*.
Carrer de l'Unió 15. Tel: 71 16 34.

CRAFTS
Artesanias
Ceramics, china, glass.
Carrer de l'Unió 13. Tel: 72 42 99.
Alpargatería Llinas
Straw-woven goods.
Carrer de Sant Miquel 43. Tel: 71 76 96.
Cesteria del Centro
Straw-woven baskets and other articles.
Passeig des Born 18. Tel: 72 45 33.
Ninot Tauro
Puppets, dolls, unusual ornaments.
Plaça La Llotja. Tel: 72 35 24.

FOOD AND DRINK
Colmado Santo Domingo
Abundance of Mallorcan delicacies.
Carrer de Sant Domingo 5.
La Montaña
Cheeses and sausages of all kinds.
Carrer de Jaume II 29. Tel: 71 25 95.

GLASS
Gordiola
Vidrio soplado (hand-blown glass).
Carrer de Victoria 2. Tel: 71 15 41.

HOME FURNISHINGS
Arte España
Quality crafts and home products from
all over Spain.
Passeig Mallorca 17. Tel: 72 82 64.
Casa Bet Merceria
Cotton, lace, belts, tapestries.
Carrer de Bosseria 6. Tel: 72 20 69.
Casa Buades
Quality ornaments and *objets d'art.*
Plaça Cort 13. Tel: 21 21 40.
Dana
Hand-embroidered cloths, table linen,
blouses.
Carrer de Puigdorfila 5. Tel: 72 42 82.
Herederos de Vicente Juan
Roba de llengues (see page 144).
Carrer de Sant Nicolau 10.
Tel: 72 17 73.
El Baul Magico
Children's furniture and toys.
Carrer de Morey 4. Tel: 72 82 20.
Mirador Lenceria
Tablecloths, lace, mats.
Carrer de Conquistador 5. Tel: 72 18 49.

HYPERMARKETS
Continente
Avinguda Cardenal Rossell, Coll Rebassa.
Tel: 26 67 00.
Pryca
Avinguda General Riera 156–72.
Tel: 29 74 00.

PEARLS AND JEWELLERY
Carrer d'Argenteria and Carrer de
Plateria are full of jewellery shops.
Perlas Orquídea
Artificial pearls.
Plaça Rei Joan Carles I. Tel: 71 57 97.

A shrine to *sobrasada* (spiced sausage) in Carrer
de Santo Domingo, Palma

SOUVENIRS
La Concha
Dolls, ceramics, glassware, *siurells.*
Carrer de Jaume II, 20. Tel: 71 15 41.

STAMPS
Pampa
Carrer de Conquistador 3. Tel: 72 33 82.

Shopping Around the Island

ANTIQUES
Antiguedades Gaul
Avinguda de Rei Jaume II, Inca.
Tel: 50 28 48.
H T Schmidt
Carrer d'Antonio Maura 42, Pollença.
Tel: 53 29 99.

CERAMICS
Art de Mallorca
Carrer de Convent 4, Manacor.
Tel: 55 07 90.
Artesania Goddy
Carrer del Pins, Port d'Alcúdia.
Tel: 54 80 23.
Artesania Goddy
Carrer de Joan Sebastià Elcano 7,
Port de Pollença. Tel: 53 03 43.

GLASS
Casa Gordiola
See pages 113 and 144.
Carretera Manacor, km19, Algaida.
Tel: 66 50 46.
Lafiore
Carretera Vieja de Valldemossa 1,
S'Esgleieta. Tel: 61 01 40.

HYPERMARKETS
Gigante
Chain of giant stores.
Avinguda Bienvenidos, Cala d'Or.
Tel: 65 80 24; Avinguda de las Palmeres,
Sa Coma. Tel: 81 08 35; Avinguda Jaume
I, Santa Ponça. Tel: 69 29 50.

LEATHER GOODS
Inca is the centre of Mallorca's leather
industry.
Yanko
Carretera Palma–Alcúdia km27.
Tel: 50 04 00.

Mar-Piel
Avinguda Lluc. Tel: 50 37 79.

OLIVE-WOOD GOODS
Oliv-Art
Carretera Palma km47, Manacor.
Tel: 55 02 30.

PEARLS AND JEWELLERY
L'Or de Mallorca
Carrer de Blanquerna 10, Valldemossa.
Tel: 61 61 14.
Perlas Majórica
Via Majorca 52, Manacor. Tel: 55 02 00.
Perlas Manacor
Avinguda Riche, Manacor. Tel: 55 03 00.
Perlas Orquídea
Plaça Ramón Llull 14–15, Manacor.
Tel: 55 04 00.

MARKETS
Mallorca's markets are worth visiting for
their local character as much as for the
articles on sale. Local fruit is well worth
buying, and you may see some pottery or
leather goods that appeal. Beware
pickpockets and importuning ladies
selling flowers and tablecloths.

Of the regular weekly markets listed
below, the most worth seeking out are
the daily produce market in Palma's
Plaça de l'Olivar, the traditional
Wednesday livestock-and-everything
jamboree in Sineu, and the sprawling
Thursday morning market in Inca.
Unless otherwise stated, all are morning
markets (and are usually fading fast by
2pm).

PALMA
Plaça del Olivar
This is a good place to buy the best of

local and imported produce as well as specialities like _sobrasada_ and cheese from Menorca. In addition to fruit and vegetables there is a meat hall upstairs, a fish hall to the side, several _tapas_ bars and even a small public library.
Monday to Saturday 8.30am–2pm.

Rastrillo (Flea Market)
Junk, secondhand household goods, reject china, lurid plastic toys and the odd antique. Expect to barter for your bargains.
Lower part of Avinguda G A Villalonga.
Saturday morning 8am–2pm.

Plaça Major
Crafts stalls selling jewellery, souvenirs, folk art.
Monday, Friday and Saturday 10am–2pm.

WEST OF PALMA
Andratx Wednesday
Calvià Monday

NORTHWEST
Alaró Friday afternoon
Binisalem Friday
Bunyola Saturday
Campanet Tuesday
Consell Thursday
Santa Maria Sunday
Sencelles Wednesday
Sóller Saturday
Valldemossa Sunday

NORTHEAST
Alcúdia Tuesday and Sunday
Artà Tuesday
Cala Rajada Saturday
Can Picafort Tuesday afternoon
Capdepera Wednesday
Costitx Saturday
Inca Thursday
Lloseta Saturday

Stall selling table linen in Palma's Rastrillo, a flea market held every Saturday

Llubí Tuesday
Maria de la Salut Friday
Montuïri Monday
Muro Sunday
Pollença Sunday
Port de Pollença Wednesday
Sa Pobla Sunday
Sant Llorenç des Cardassar Thursday
Santa Margalida Tuesday and Saturday
Selva Wednesday
Sineu Wednesday
Son Servera Friday
Vilafranca de Bonany Wednesday

SOUTH
Algaida Friday
Campos Thursday
Felanitx Sunday
Llucmajor Wednesday and Sunday
Manacor Monday
Porreres Tuesday
Porto Cristo Sunday
S'Arenal Thursday
Sa Colònia de Sant Jordi Wednesday
Santanyí Saturday
Ses Salines Thursday.

Entertainment

In the resorts the music, shows and nightlife are geared to the international tastes of the briefly visiting holidaymaker. Alongside this popular entertainment, the Mallorcans have their own cultural activities, including a busy calendar of religious and secular celebrations.

WHAT'S ON

Events, a free quarterly in English with an up-to-date listing of the main sporting and cultural activities in the Balearic Islands, is available from tourist offices. Programmes and topical events are also advertised in local papers and tourist-orientated publications (see page 184).

Bear in mind that the Spanish like to party late, and local *fiestas* may not really get going till well after the times advertised. In July and August many open-air concerts and musical events will not start before 10pm. The choice of bars, clubs and discos is dramatically curtailed out of season, but there is always something going on.

ART GALLERIES

Mallorca has a buoyant art scene, and several art galleries have bars and bookshops attached – notably Fundació La Caixa and Sa Nostra in Palma. A free bi-monthly leaflet issued by Associació Independent de Galeries d'Art de Balears gives details of what some galleries are exhibiting.

In Palma:
4 Gats
Carrer de Sant Sebastià 2. Tel: 72 64 93.
Fundació Barceló
Casa del Marqués de Requer, Carrer de Sant Jaume 4. Tel: 72 24 67.
Fundació La Caixa
See page 35.
Sa Nostra
Carrer de Concepció 12. Tel: 72 52 10.

Around the island:
Maior
Plaça Major 4, Pollença. Tel: 53 00 95.
Pedrona Torrens
Carrer de Sant Jaume 1, Alcúdia.
Tel: 54 83 24.
S'Estació
Carrer d'Estació, Sineu. Tel: 52 07 50.

British pubs, German bars: there's no shortage of watering-holes in the resorts

Floorshow at the Casino Mallorca, where you can wine, dine and lose you shirt

BARS AND PUBS

All the resorts have a strip of wall-to-wall pubs and bars. In Palma the greatest concentration is around Plaça Gomila in the Es Terreno district. The area is quite seedy, and popular with the US Navy. In the city centre, Carrer de Apuntadores is always lively.

CASINO

Mallorca has one casino, Casino Mallorca. This is combined with the Casino Palladium, which offers dinner and variety shows and is available as an organised excursion. Gaming includes roulette, blackjack and slot machines. A jacket and tie for men and your passport are required.

Urbanización Sol de Mallorca, at the end of the motorway to Andratx (turn off at Cala Figuera), Calvià. Tel: 13 00 00. Open: daily 8pm–4am.

CINEMAS

Programmes and times are advertised in the local newspapers, and films are usually dubbed into Castilian Spanish. Cinemas (*cine*) seem to be the only places to go for many young Mallorcans, and are often packed out for the latest Hollywood releases. The following are all in Palma.

Chaplin Multicines
Carrer de Josep Darder Metge. Tel: 27 76 62.

Nuevo Hispania
Carrer de Benito Pons 4. Tel: 27 04 75.

Sala Augusta
Avinguda Joan March 2. Tel: 75 20 55.

Salón Rialto
Carrer de Sant Feliu 5. Tel: 72 12 45.

Hotels and bars in the resorts also screen English language videos and TV programmes.

DISCOS AND NIGHTCLUBS

There are over 150 discothèques and nightclubs in Mallorca, providing sounds for everyone from teenyboppers to the young at heart. Though the wilder scene is on the neighbouring island of Ibiza, several establishments have earned a reputation for their extravagant décor and light shows. The best alternative discos tend to come and go, or at least change their names to suggest they are moving with the times. To find the beat you need to ask around in bars and clothes shops, or chat up the beach Adonises handing out flyers. Nightclubs, catering to refined spenders and dressers, are often part of a luxury hotel.

In Palma:
Indigo
Latin and 1960s music.
Carrer de Corb Marí 7.
Factory
Young crowd in an old factory.
Plaça Mediterráneo.
Luna
Boppy in-crowd.
Ca'n Barbara, Passeig Marítim 42.
Clan
Teenagers evolving into post-teenagers.
Plaça del Vapor, Es Jonquet.
Tel: 45 86 69.
Tito's.
Top-rate nightclub for all.
Plaça Gomila 3. Tel: 73 76 42.

Elsewhere:
BCM
4,000 capacity, state-of-the-art light show.
Avinguda S'Olivera, Magaluf.
Tel: 13 06 82.

Mallorcan dances in traditional costume are a feature of *fiestas* and folklore shows

Dhraa
Designer disco with international sounds.
Carretera Porto Cristo–Cala Millor km4.
Tel: 57 09 31.

FOLKLORE AND DINNER SHOWS

Exhibitions of Mallorcan music and dance are staged regularly in the summer at La Granja and Valldemossa (see pages 53 and 80), and often coincide with coach excursions. Floorshows, barbecues, pirate adventures and medieval banquets can also be booked through your hotel.

Es Foguero
Dinner and floorshow.
Carretera Palma–Santanyí km11.
Tel: 71 26 99.
Es Foguero Palace
Dinner and floorshow.
Carretera Alcúdia–Sa Pobla. Tel: 89 02 85.
Son Amar
Dinner and floorshow.
Carretera de Sóller km10.8, Bunyola.
Tel: 75 36 14.

Pirate Adventure
Dinner and yo-ho-ho.
Carretera La Porassa, Magaluf.
Tel: 13 04 11.

HOTEL ENTERTAINMENT
Hotels like to keep you in their clutches, and the high-class ones put on quality live music to help guests run up the bar bill with a devil-may-care grin. Non-residents are welcome to join the parties, so if your own multilingual bingo caller is too much, try the monosyllabic magician next door. Programmes are usually posted up in foyers, with regular spots each day of the week. Don't be surprised if performances start later than advertised.

MUSICAL EVENTS
Concerts and music festivals are staged in Mallorca throughout the year, including a programme of musical and popular events in the resorts between November and April. All the following are in Palma unless stated otherwise. Ask at a tourist office for more details of the dates and programme.
January: classical and light music for Sant Sebastià fiesta.
March: international week of organ music.
March–June: spring opera season at Teatre Principal.
July: international folk dancing at Sóller.
July–August: international music festival in Pollença and Chopin festival at Valldemossa. Summer serenades in Castell de Bellver and music festivals in Deià, Artà and Santuari de Cura (Puig de Randa).
September–October: festival of classical music in Bunyola.
October: week of organ concerts in local churches.

Mallorca's international disco scene

THEATRES AND CONCERT HALLS
Auditòrium
Passeig Marítim 18, Palma. Tel: 73 47 35. Tickets sold 10am–2pm and 4–9pm.
Teatre Principal
Carrer de la Riera 2, Palma. Tel: 72 55 48.
Ses Voltes
Parc de la Mar, Palma. Tel: 71 42 38.
Other venues for irregular music and dance events are the Bendinat Golf Club (west of Palma), Castell de Bellver (Palma), Son Marroig, Valldemossa, Sa Calobra (all three in the northwest of the island), Casa March gardens (near Cala Rajada in the northeast), and in churches and monasteries around the island.

THE *DAILY BEE*
World news, sports reports and local issues are all covered by the English-language *Majorca Daily Bulletin*, affectionately known as the *Daily Bee*. Now over 30 years old, the newspaper is a venerable example of the outspoken, visitor-pleasing publications found in many holiday destinations. Serious reporting is always spiced with the sensational and quirky, be it a story on the burial of a Belgian horse standing upright in its coffin to adverts for O-Tony the Spanish Masseur. At 100 *pesetas*, it would be rude not to try it.

DANCING WITH THE DEVIL

The Spanish are addicted to *fiestas*, and in Mallorca scarcely a week goes by without a celebration of some kind. The inspiration for most festivities is religious, but rural traditions and historic events on the island make their mark too. Animals, fish, grapes, sausages and even melons are all cause for a *fiesta* here, while heroic resistance against invading Turkish pirates in the mid-16th century is still remembered in Sóller and Pollença with mock battles between Moors and Christians.

Dimonis (devils) are among the most eye-catching characters that dance through Mallorcan *fiestas*. Once banned by the Church, devils now appear at many *fiestas*, hurling firecrackers and lewdly tempting saints and spectators alike. One of the island's oldest rituals, played out annually by dancers at Montuïri, features a shabbily dressed devil with horns and a cow-bell being danced into submission by a Lady, who concludes her conquest by placing a triumphant foot on the defeated embodiment of evil. In a *fiesta* at Santa Margalida anarchic devils infiltrate a procession of villagers dressed in rural costume, snatching their *gerres* (pitchers) which are then smashed at the feet of Mallorca's own saint, Santa Catalina Thomás.

Some *fiestas* begin on the eve

Red devils: the island's festivals are renowned
for their colour and drama

(*revelta*) of a local saint's day, when
ceremonial bonfires (*foguerons)* are lit.
At Sa Pobla, where the Revelta de Sant
Antoni dates back to 1365, the
celebrants tuck into specially made eel
and spinach pie and dance to traditional
music played on bagpipe, flute and
drum. In Pollença the local braves bring
a pine tree down from the mountains,
which is made into a soapy pole for the
townsfolk to climb.

The *fiesta* calendar is at its busiest
between June and September. For the
non-religious visitor, country fairs and
the more theatrical *fiestas* will be the
most rewarding events to track down.
Instead of standing around waiting for
the parade to begin (it is bound to be
late), get in a bar, have a few drinks and
ask the waiter where is the best place to
stand – and when. Then have a devil of
a good time.

Festivals

JANUARY

5th: Cabalgata de Los Reyes Magos
(Cavalcade of the Three Kings). In Palma
the Kings arrive by boat then proceed
through the town accompanied by toy-
laden lorries. The next day, Epiphany, is
when Spanish children receive their
Christmas presents.

16th–17th: Sant Antoni Abat. The
patron saint of animals is honoured with
bonfires, music, dancing and processions
of animals brought for blessing.

20th: Festa de Sant Sebastià (patron
saint of Palma and Alcúdia) is celebrated
with music and bonfires. In Palma a week
of cultural festivities culminates with a
celebration in Plaça Mayor on the 19th.

FEBRUARY

February is Carnival month, with
celebrations all around the island. In
Palma it is known as **Sa Rúa**, with
decorated floats and costumed parades on
Carnival Sunday. **Darrer Dies** (Last
Days) in Montuïri involves fancy dress,
stalls, wine, food and bonfires.

MARCH/APRIL

Semana Santa (Easter) is a serious
religious occasion. On Palm Sunday olive
and palm branches are carried to church
and used to decorate doors and balconies.
The religious processions for Easter Week
reach a visual and emotional peak on
Maundy Thursday and Good Friday
when masked penitents in pointed hoods
march around Palma's streets carrying
torches and holy relics. The Good Friday
processions in Sineu and Pollença are
particularly dramatic.

18 April: Festa del Angel. In the forest
around Castell de Bellver.

MAY/JUNE

8–10 May: Ses Valentes Dones (The
Valiant Women) commemorates the
defeat of Turkish pirates in 1561 in which
two local women were outstandingly
brave. A battle between Christians and
Moors is re-enacted by local youths in
Port de Sóller, with the survivors repeating
the affray later in the evening in Sóller
town.

Corpus Christi: Religious celebration in
honour of the Blessed Sacrament.

13 June: Sant Antoni de Juny. Local
fiesta in Artà with dancing and figures
dressed as horses.

24 June: Festa d'es Sol Que Balla (Feast
of the Dancing Sun). Agricultural show in
Sant Joan. **Festes de Sant Joan,** local
fiesta in Muro with bullfights.

28–9 June: Festes de Sant Pere. Port
d'Alcúdia pays homage to St Peter, patron
saint of fishermen.

30 June: Romería de Sant Marçal.
Marratxí celebrates its patron with a
pilgrimage and sale of *siurells.*
Country fairs in Campos, Sineu, Felanitx,
Sencelles and Manacor.

JULY

**2nd: Romería a la Virgen de la
Victoria.** Pilgrimage from Alcúdia to
Ermita de la Victoria.

16th: Festes de la Virgen del Carmen.
Local *fiestas* in Port d'Andratx, Cala
Ratjada, Port de Pollença and Port de
Sóller.

27th–28th: Passejada d'es Bou and
Carro Triunfal. In Valldemossa, as part
of the cult of Santa Catalina Thomás a
bull is led through the streets. Next day
sees a triumphal procession of carts with
a local girl dressed as the saint.

AUGUST

2nd: Festa de Nostra Senyora de los Angeles. Pollença's local *fiesta* includes a mock fight between Christians and Moors.

10th: Festa de Sant Llorenç. Selva's patron saint is honoured.

24th: Sant Bartomeu. Capdepera remembers St Bartholomew with horse racing. Devil dances in Montuïri.

28th: Sant Agustín. Dancing and horsey antics in Felanitx.

29th: Sant Joan. Sant Joan celebrates its eponymous patron with dancing and Balearic slinging.

Pilgrimage on foot from Palma to Lluc.

SEPTEMBER

21st: Festa de Sant Mateu. *Fiesta* in Bunyola.

First Sunday: devils-versus-saints procession in Santa Margalida.

Second Sunday: melon *fiesta* in Vilafranca de Bonany.

Last Sunday: Binisalem has a grape and wine festival. Country fairs in Montuïri and Artà.

OCTOBER

Third Sunday: **Festa d'es Botifarró.** *Botifarró* sausage festival in Sant Joan.

16th: La Beateta. Costumed procession in Palma celebrating Santa Catalina Thomás. Country fairs in Alcúdia, Campos, Felanitx, Porreres and Llucmajor. Raft race in Porto Portals.

NOVEMBER

Third Thursday: **Dijous Bò.** Major agricultural show in Inca.

30th: Festa de Sant Andreu. *Fiesta* in Santanyí.

DECEMBER

25th: Navidad. Carol concerts and Nativity scenes are a feature of the Mallorcan Christmas.

31st: Festa de l'Estendard. Palma remembers Jaume I's capture of the city in 1229.

Ask at a tourist office for up-to-date information as dates sometimes change.

Festive antics in Montuïri

Children

Mallorca is most suitable for children. Besides offering plenty of sandy beaches with safe, shallow water, the island's resorts all have purpose-built activities and amusements to bankrupt Mum and Dad. In the high season facilities can get stretched and care is required with the strong sun, but Mallorca has everything you need for a family holiday by the sea.

Water parks like Aquacity in S'Arenal are always popular with children

BEACHES
The following beaches are ideal for children.

West of Palma
Santa Ponça: broad family beach (page 58).
Magaluf: busy but plenty to do (page 56).

Northeast
Port de Pollença: easygoing atmosphere (page 104).
Port d'Alcúdia: clear, shallow water (page 104).

Platja de Muro: backed by dunes and low pines (page 104).
Cala Millor: wide golden sands (page 92).
Sa Coma: popular beach, popular resort (page 92).

South
Can Pastilla: classic holiday beach (page 116).
S'Arenal: unbridled seaside fun (page 126).
Cala Llombards: small, shallow cove (page 129).
Cala Pi: sheltered, out-of-the-way cove (page 128).

RESORTS
Children's facilities lean towards physical activities rather than the mind-stimulating amusements common in the US. Besides the beach, swimming pools and indoor games, large hotels put on children's shows, perhaps a magician or clowns, as part of their entertainment programme. Funfairs and circuses also visit Mallorca. Beach games, sports and fishing equipment can be bought in seaside shops, and bicycles with child-seats rented. Some riding clubs have small ponies suitable for young riders, and a mini-golf course is rarely far away.

WHAT NOW?
There is always something for children to do on Mallorca. Ask at your hotel reception about the entertainment available

in your locality. For boat trips see page 134, for spectator sports and sporting facilities pages 160–3. Some cultural events, like Carnival or the Porto Portals Raft Race, will appeal to youngsters. The following attractions are particularly relevant to children.

Palma

Es Casal des Tren: in the courtyard of the 15th-century Oratori de Sant Pere, this cafeteria-style restaurant has a child-mesmerising model train and carriages running on tracks set high above the head. Carrer de Sindicat is pedestrianised and full of shops.
Carrer de Sindicat 21. Tel: 72 86 53.
Palma–Sóller train ride see page 82.

West of Palma

Aquapark: popular waterpark with slides and a go-kart track next door.
On the Magaluf–Cala Figuera road.
Tel: 68 08 11. Open: daily 15 April–
31 October 10am–8pm. Admission charge.
El Dorado: Wild West experience with show.
On the Magaluf–Cala Figuera road.
Tel: 13 08 49. Daily show at noon.
Monday to Saturday visits 1–7pm (3pm Sunday). Admission charge.
Golf Fantasia: miniature golf among caves, waterfalls and tropical gardens.
Carrer de Tenis, Palma Nova.
Tel: 69 23 49. Admission charge.
Marineland: performing dolphins, sea-lions and parrots. See page 53.
Nemo Submarines: underwater exploration by mini-submarine.
Carrer de Pedro Vaquer Ramis (on the corner of Carrer de Galeon), Magaluf.
Tel: 13 03 44.

Northwest

Aqualandia and **El Foro de Mallorca**: waterpark with a wax museum.
On the Palma–Inca road at km25, Binisalem. Tel: 51 12 28. Open: daily 9am–8pm (7pm winter). Admission charge.

Northeast

Hidropark: water slides, chutes and kamikaze slides.
Avinguda Inglaterra, Port d'Alcúdia.
Tel: 54 70 72. Open: daily 10am–7pm. Admission charge.
Reserva Africana: drive-round animal park. See page 105.

South

Acuario de Mallorca: aquarium near the Coves del Drac. See page 124.
Aquacity: waterpark with slides, chutes and amusements. See page 126.
Exotic-Parque Los Pajaros: Parrot Park near Cales de Mallorca. See page 115.
Son Gual Parc Prehistòric: plastic monsters in the bushes. See page 127. Tourist trains run along the seafront between Can Pastilla and S'Arenal, and in Cala d'Or between the town centre and marina.

Monster fun: a resident of the Son Gual Parc Prehistòric smiles for the camera

Sport

*T*he range of sports available on Mallorca is wide. Watersports, sailing and golf are the main attraction for visitors, while football, basketball and cycling appeal to many Mallorcans. In summer the heat and strong sun should be taken seriously, but facilities and activities are usually available in the evening. Enquire at your hotel reception or visit a tourist office to find out what sporting opportunities are close to where you are staying.

ADVENTURE SPORTS

The Serra de Tramuntana is featured in specialist guidebooks to climbing in Spain, and shops selling mountain climbing and adventure equipment stock maps and routes.

Escuela de Vuelo Ultraligero
(microlight flying)
Aeródromo de Binissalem, Camí de Son Roig km2. Tel: 41 38 05.
Gem (mountaineering club)
Carrer d'Imprenta 1, Palma. Tel: 71 13 14.
Real Aeroclub de Baleares (flying and parachute jumps)
Aeródromo de Son Bonet, Marratxí. Tel: 60 01 14.

BASKETBALL

Mallorca has a top division basketball (*baloncesto*) team, Prohaci Mallorca, who play in the 5,000-seater Palau Municipal d'Esportes.
Camí La Vileta, Palma. Tel: 73 99 41.

BOWLING
Interbowling Club
Avinguda Joan Miró, Palma. Tel: 73 81 45.
Bowling Palma
Carrer de Cardenal Rossell 64, Coll d'en Rabassa. Tel: 26 87 54.

BULLFIGHTING

The Spanish consider the bullfight more of an artistic performance than a spectator sport. In Mallorca bullfighting is still held in high esteem by its *aficionados*, but it does not have the status or following associated with the *corridas* held on the mainland. If you have never been to a bullfight, Mallorca is probably not the best place to experiment: for the traditional drama and spectacle, it is better to go to one of the great arenas, for instance in Seville or Madrid.

A season of bullfights takes place every summer in Palma's Plaça de Toros, and there are also bullrings in Inca, Muro and Alcúdia where fights are often staged to coincide with a local celebration. During the bullfight season posters and newspaper advertisements appear with details of the programme and how to buy tickets. Seats in the sun (*sol*) are cheaper than those in the shade (*sombra*). Organised excursions are sometimes arranged, for example to Alcúdia where mock bullfights with exhibitions of dressage are staged every Thursday at 6pm in the summer.

Plaça de Toros
Avinguda Gaspar B Arquitecte 32, Palma. Tel: 75 26 39.

CYCLING

For leisure cycling see page 135. Spring is the main season for competitive cycling when a round-island race is staged. There is a velodrome in Palma's Palau Municipal d'Esports (see **Sports Centres**, page 163).

Federación Balear di Ciclismo
Carrer de Francesc Faiol i Juan 2, Palma. Tel: 20 83 62.

DIVING
There are several scuba-diving clubs and schools on the island that take advantage of the clear waters around the Mallorcan coast.

Federación Balear di Actividades Subacuaticas
Carrer de Pere d'Alcàntara Penya 13, Palma. Tel: 46 33 15.

Aquamarine Diving
Port d'Andratx. Tel: 67 43 76.

Unidad Costa Norte
Port Adriano, Calvià. Tel: 10 26 76.

Scuba Palma
Via Jaume I 84, Santa Ponça. Tel: 69 02 66.

FISHING
Porto Cristo is a favourite spot for underwater fishing and used for world championships. Licences are required for fishing in Mallorcan waters. For sports or underwater fishing contact:

Comandancia de Marina
Moll Vell 1, Palma. Tel: 71 13 71.

For trout and carp fishing in the mountain reservoirs at Gorg Blau and Cúber contact:

ICONA
Passatge de Guillermo de Torrela 1, Palma. Tel: 71 74 40.

For information on fishing and a list of regulations contact:

Direcció General de Pesca i Cultius Marins
Passeig de Joan XXII 6, Palma. Tel: 71 10 23.

FOOTBALL
Mallorca is home to two teams in the Spanish football league, Real Mallorca and Atlético Baleares. Matches are normally played on Sundays during the season at Palma's Lluis Sitjar stadium.
Plaça Barcelona. Tel: 45 21 11.

Bullfighting in Mallorca is held in high esteem

GOLF

Golf is extremely popular with visitors to Mallorca – the best known clubs are at Santa Ponça and Son Vida. Competitions are frequently held, including the annual Balearic Open. Golfing holidays to Mallorca can be arranged as a package, and golf passes, giving access to all the island's clubs, can be bought. All courses have 18 holes unless stated otherwise. Two more are currently under construction.

Go for the greens at Son Vida golf course

West of Palma
Golf de Poniente. Tel: 13 01 48.
Golf Santa Ponça I. Tel: 69 02 11.
Real Golf Bendinat. Tel: 40 52 00 (9 holes).
Son Vida Club de Golf. Tel: 79 12 10.

Northeast
Canyamel Golf Club. Tel: 56 44 77.
Capdepera Golf Club Roca Viva. Tel: 56 58 74.
Club de Golf de Pollença. Tel: 53 32 16 (9 holes).
Club de Golf Son Servera. Tel: 56 78 02 (9 holes).

South
Club de Golf Vall d'Or. Tel: 83 70 01.
Federación Balear de Golf
Avinguda Jaume III, 17. Palma.
Tel: 72 27 53.

GREYHOUND RACING

There is one track, the Canodròmo in Camí de Jesus in Palma (tel: 29 00 12). Races start at 4.30pm, daily except Wednesday.

HORSE RACING

Trotting races (*carreras*) are popular with a dedicated section of Mallorcan society. There are two race tracks, near Palma and Manacor. Competition is keen with betting by a centralised tote system. Race meetings normally take place on Sundays at 9pm between June and September and at 4pm for the rest of the year.
Hipódromo de Son Pardo
Carretera Palma–Sóller km3.
Tel: 75 40 31.
Hipódromo de Manacor
Esplá, Carretera Manacor–Artà.
Tel: 55 00 33.

RIDING

Classes for beginners and advanced riders are available at several centres around the island.
Club Escuela d'Equitación de Mallorca
Carretera de Palma–Sóller km12, Bunyola.
Tel: 61 31 57.
Equitación Rancho la Romana
Carretera d'Andratx, Peguera.
Tel: 68 52 90.

SAILING

Mallorca is a prominent Mediterranean sailing and yachting centre with over 40 marinas. The Club Nautico (Nautical Club) in each port is the focus of this activity. Several resident companies offer yacht charter services. National and international competitions include the King's Cup and Princess Sofia Cup, and in August historic sailing boats take part in the Trofeo Conde de Barcelona.

Have fun while you see the island – sailing boats for hire in Port de Pollença

There are sailing schools at Peguera and S'Arenal, and dinghies can be hired in many resorts.

Federación Balear de Vela
Cala Nova, Carrer de Joan Miró, Palma. Tel: 40 24 12.

SPORTS CENTRES
Some hotels have saunas and fitness centres, while those catering specifically for sports enthusiasts have gyms and a programme of exercise classes and tuition. Mallorca has many municipal sports centres (Palau Municipal d'Esports) with a high standard of equipment (football pitch, swimming pool, gym, tennis courts, athletics track). They are also the venue for many sports competitions. Facilities are particularly good in the Calvià area, with centres in Calvià, Magaluf, Peguera and Santa Ponça.

Palau Municipal d'Esports de Palma
Camí La Vileta. Tel: 73 99 41.

TENNIS
Many hotels have their own courts and the larger resorts have tennis centres providing additional facilities. Tuition in English is available and some courts are floodlit. You may have to book a day or two ahead at peak times.

Federación Balear de Tenis
Carrer de Posadade la Real 6, Palma. Tel: 72 09 56.

TRADITIONAL SPORTS
The ancient slinging skill of the Balearic *hondero* (see page 33) is still practised by enthusiasts in *tiro con honda* competitions.

Federación de Tiro Con Honda
Carrer de Oms, Palma. Tel: 72 62 50.

WATERSPORTS
Windsurfing tuition and board hire can be found in many resorts, and jet-skiing and water-skiing in larger ones.

Federación Balear de Motonautica (motor-boats)
Carrer de Francesc Suau 2, Palma. Tel: 20 61 14.

Ski Club Calanova (water-skiing)
Carrer de D Eugenio Molina, Magaluf. Tel: 13 09 65.

Food and Drink

*T*he Mallorcans, along with the million visitors a year from the Spanish mainland, enjoy a good meal out. Traditionally based on fish, pork and lamb, the islanders' cuisine is at heart simple, robust fare. Now catering to international tastes, Mallorca's restaurants run the full range from terrific to terrible. Price is no automatic guarantee of quality and, as with all mass holiday destinations, you have to be selective.

MALLORCAN SPECIALITIES

The pig lies behind two of Mallorca's best known comestibles. *Sobrasada* is a blood-red pork-based sausage, often spiced with peppers and made to the butcher's personal recipe. Try them as *tapas*, the small dishes of food served in many Spanish bars. Pigs also provide the lard essential to the delicious *ensaimada,* a light, spiral, sugar-dusted pastry sometimes filled with 'angel's hair'

(pumpkin jam) – a favourite way to start the Mallorcan day. Sold in dartboard-sized octagonal boxes, they make interesting and conveniently light presents to take home.

Some restaurants specialise in *cuina Mallorquína* (Mallorcan cooking) – the best are in Palma or out in the countryside. In the latter, service may be slow as your food is being freshly prepared. The following dishes often appear on their menus.

Arroz brut: ('dirty rice'), usually a savoury saffron-flavoured soup with small pieces of meat and vegetables

Arroz negro: rice blackened with squid ink

Botifarró: highly seasoned cured pork and blood sausage

Caracoles: snails, often served with garlic and mayonnaise

Empanadas: pastry-covered pie with meat and vegetables

Escaldun: stew made with chicken, potatoes and almonds

Espinagada: eel and spinach pie

Frito Mallorquín: fry-up with liver, kidney and peppers

Lechona asada: roast suckling pig

Lomo con setas: fried pork with mushrooms

Pa amb oli: bread smeared with olive

Ensaimadas, spirals of light, sweet pastry, are a Mallorcan speciality

oil, garlic and tomatoes
Sopa Mallorquína: vegetable soup with bread and garlic
Tordos con col: thrushes wrapped in cabbage
Tumbet: a seasoned dish similar to ratatouille, made with red and green peppers, aubergines and potatoes.

Other dishes feature rabbit (*conejo*), chicken (*pollo*), lamb (*cordero*) and kidneys (*riñones*). Meat cooked *al horno* is slow-roasted in a brick oven.

Fish
Good quality fresh fish is no longer cheap. Restaurants often have the day's catch out on display for customers to make their choice. The fish is sold by weight – a large rarity can be alarmingly expensive, but a good waiter will always tell you the price before it hits the pan. It is quite acceptable to ask for a sizeable fish to be divided between two. Menus in fish restaurants often include the following dishes.
Arroz marinera: fish soup with rice
Calderata langosta: pieces of lobster in a tomato sauce
Gambas: prawns
Lubina con sal: sea bass baked in a mountain of rock salt
Puntillas: baby squid
Salmonetes: red mullet
Sardinas a la plancha: grilled sardines.

Cakes and Desserts
Beside the ubiquitous *flan* (crème caramel) and *helados* (ice-cream), better restaurants will stock *Menorquina* and other brands of frozen desserts, such as

lemons stuffed with lemon ice-cream. Cakes featuring almonds are a safe bet, such as *tarta de almendras* (almond tart). The best cheese made in the Balearic Islands comes from Menorca.

Water
Tap water in Mallorca is safe to drink but can taste salty. It is better to drink bottled water, which is not expensive and can be bought in 5 litre containers from supermarkets. Water with bubbles is *agua con gas*, without *sin gas*.

Food for all in the resorts (above); fish in Palma's Plaça del l'Olivar market (below)

DRINKS
Wine and Beer
Mallorcan wine is worth trying, particularly the more expensive reds from the José Ferrer label. Wines from Binisalem, the island's viticultural centre, have recently gained DO status (Denominación d'Origen), a sign of their improving quality. Although foreign grape varieties have been introduced, all red wines from here include at least 50 per cent of the local Manto Negro (Black Cloak) grape. Those marked *vino de crianza* have been aged in oak casks and are at least two years old.

Wines imported from other regions of Spain are always available, along with many beers from around Europe. Beer (*cerveza*), the first and only Spanish word learnt by an over-publicised minority of visitors to Mallorca, is cheaper if bought draught – ask for *una caña*. If you get carried away, *boquerones* (anchovies), available in any *tapas* bar, are a good hangover cure.

Spirits
Mallorca's contribution to the befuddling choice of Spanish spirits and liqueurs are *hierbas*. These are aromatic herb- and aniseed-based liqueurs which come *seco* (dry) or *dulce* (sweet). Free tasting of the various flavours, such as those sold under the Tunel label, are a feature of excursions visiting *bodegas* or large souvenir emporia. *Palo*, a dark aperitif made from crushed and fermented carob

Have a drink: the well-stocked bar in the Celler Ca'n Amer restaurant, Inca

seeds, will appeal to the intrepid experimenter.

The best and most palatable spirit to take home is gin made on Menorca – the Xoriguer brands come in a distinctive brown bottle with a windmill label. The production of gin on that island is a legacy of the British presence there for much of the 18th century.

Non-alcoholic drinks

With so many orange trees on the island, freshly-squeezed orange juice (*zumo de naranja*) is an appropriate drink, particularly in the Sóller area. Try it mixed with lemon (*limon*) for additional tang, or refreshingly packed with ice (*granizado*). Some bars, like **Abaco** in Palma (Carrer de Sant Joan 1), make a feature of their juicy combinations. *Horchata*, a milky drink made from almonds, is also sold. Coffee comes black (*café solo*), white (*café con leche*), with only a little milk (*café cortado*), laced with brandy (*café carajillo*) or iced (*granizado de café*). By comparison tea (*té*) is invariably a simple marriage of hot water and tea-bag – teapots are as rare as skiers in Mallorca.

WHERE TO EAT

In the resorts the choice of cuisine and dining venues verges on the exhausting. Many restaurants have similar menus offering adequate but unmemorable international fare. The Spanish employ a fork system to grade their restaurants, but this can be ignored completely. Instead, look for signs of quality. Has the computer-printed menu been there since last winter? Do the waiters look as if they will be proud to serve you? Are there any Spanish diners inside? Ask about the *especialidad del día* (speciality of the day) – not to be confused with *menú del día,* a

Palma sign: if you always keep your drink at arms length it will last longer

generally dull set meal all restaurants have to offer by law (though it can be good value in country villages).

Tapas bars get their name from the Sevillian practice of putting a lid (*tapa*) of ham on top of a glass of sherry. They can be anything from a saucer of olives to a terracotta dish of spicy meatballs. *Tapas* can easily mount up into a hefty bill, but they are a quintessential Spanish practice and a few *raciones* (portions) are a great way to snack while shopping and sightseeing in Palma. Try **La Boveda** in Plaça La Llotja.

Some restaurants describe themselves as *cellers* – like cellars, though not necessarily underground. Their hallmark is a rustic atmosphere with solid furniture and vast vats of wine lining the walls. **Celler Ca'n Amer** in Inca is a sophisticated example, and there are others in and around Carrer de Apuntadores, Palma's principal wining and dining street.

Restaurants

The symbols below are an indication of restaurant prices. The P symbol represents the cost of a 3-course meal, without wine or beer, per person.

P under 2,000 pesetas
PP under 4,000 pesetas
PPP over 4,000 pesetas

Many restaurants close, or are open on fewer days of the week, during the low season. Some take a holiday in July or August. If you are making a special journey, phone ahead to check your destination is open. A tax of 6 per cent IVA (value added tax) is added to restaurant bills.

PALMA

Asador Tierra Aranda PP
On the first floor of an old mansion, perfect if you are in a roast meat mood.
Carrer de Concepció 4, off Avinguda Jaume III. Tel: 71 42 56.

Caballito del Mar P
Seafront fish restaurant with terrace, by La Llotja.
Passeig Sagrera 5. Tel: 72 10 74.

Ca'n Carlos P
Cosy restaurant specialising in Mallorcan dishes.
Carrer de S'Aigo 5 (off Avinguda Jaume III). Tel: 71 38 69. Closed Sunday.

Casa Eduardo P
Quayside seafood restaurant, busy and noisy at lunch.
Industria Pesquera. Tel: 72 10 74. Closed Sunday, Monday.

El Pilón PP
City restaurant and well-known *tapas* bar with a more refined dining room upstairs.
Carrer de San Cayetano 12 (west of Passeig des Born). Tel: 71 75 90. Closed Sunday.

Es Parlament PP
Quiet, dignified, with mature décor and genuine Mallorcan dishes.
Carrer de Conquistador 11. Tel: 72 60 26. Closed Sunday.

Fora Vila PPP
Haute cuisine in a 5-star hotel with gardens, golf and impeccable service.
Hotel Arabella, Son Vida.
Tel: 79 99 99.

La Boveda P
Atmospheric *tapas* bar with huge wine barrels providing subliminal inspiration to imbibe.
Carrer de Boteria 3. Tel: 71 48 63.

La Lubina PP
A quayside fish restaurant that knows about fish, with dishes baked in rock salt a house speciality.
Moll Vell. Tel: 72 33 50.

Reial Club Nautic PP
Fish and ships in the Royal Yacht Club, with eye-pleasing harbour views at night.
Muelle San Pedro 1. Tel: 71 87 88.

S'Arrosseria PP
Intriguing and substantial rice dishes overlooking the seafront traffic, including several varieties of paella.
Passeig Marítim 13. Tel: 73 74 47.

Sa Volta P
Friendly *celler* restaurant, good for a

light, tasty meal.
Carrer de Apuntadores 5. No telephone.

WEST OF PALMA
BANYALBUFAR
Mar y Vent P
Family-run restaurant and hotel in a
tranquil village.
Carrer de Mayor 49. Tel: 61 80 00.

ESTELLENCS
Es Grau P
Spectacularly perched on the cliff-edge,
a popular stop if touring the northwest corner of the island. International
menu.
Mirador Ricardo Roca. Tel: 61 02 70.

GÉNOVA
Meson Ca'n Pedro PP
Typical Mallorcan dishes in a favourite
Sunday lunch venue for local families.
Snails are a house speciality.
*Carrer de Rector Vives 14. Tel: 70 21 62.
Closed Tuesday.*
Ses Coves P
Small restaurant by the caves serving
Catalan food.
Carrer de Barranc 45. Tel: 40 23 87.

PALMA NOVA
Ciro's PP
Orderly restaurant with terrace, serving
continental dishes.
Passeig del Mar. Tel: 68 10 52.

PORT D'ANDRATX
Miramar PP
Quality Mallorcan cooking in a formal
ambience, with a terrace overlooking the
seafront.
Avinguda Mateo Bosch 48. Tel: 67 16 17.
Rocamar P
Fish and Mallorcan dishes, or just have a
snack with views.

*Carrer d'Almirante Riera Alemany.
Tel: 67 12 61.*

SANTA PONÇA
Sa Masia PP
Upmarket dining in an old farmhouse.
International and Mallorcan dishes.
Carretera Andratx km19. Tel: 69 42 17.

SANT TELM
Flexas P
No-frills seafront fish restaurant looking
on to the bay.
On the seafront, no telephone.

NORTHWEST
ALARÓ
Es Puet PP
Isolated rustic gem of a barn with
blackboard menu offering meat roasted
in a wood-burning clay oven.
*See page 66. Tel: 51 00 02. Closed
Monday.*

ALFABIA
Ses Porxeres PP
Near perfect restaurant well-suited for a
long Mallorcan lunch, with the Alfabia
gardens next door to walk it off.
Carretera Sóller. Tel: 61 37 62.

DEIÀ
Mirador de Na Fordada PP
Viewpoint restaurant on the north coast;
dishes include Mallorcan staples like
arroz brut and *lomo con col* (pork and
cabbage).
Tel: 63 90 26.

FORNALUTX
Santa Marta PP
Delightful village restaurant with valley
views. Mallorcan cooking.
*Carrer de Bellavista 1. Tel: 63 19 52.
Closed Tuesday.*

INCA
Celler Ca'n Amer PP
Opposite the covered market and busy at lunchtime, a *celler* restaurant with interesting local dishes and wine poured straight from enormous vats.
Carrer den Miquel Durán 35.
Tel: 50 12 61. Closed Sunday.
Raco P
Family-run small bar-restaurant with untouristy menu.
Carrer de Dureta 1 (off Plaça Espanya).
Tel: 50 30 15.

ORIENT
L'Hermitage PPP
Part of a luxury hotel in an old manor house, ideal for country lovers with an expense account to burn.
Carretera Sollerich. Tel: 61 33 00.
Hostal de Muntanya PP
The village hub. Sit on the terrace and enjoy roast meat followed by Mallorca-grown strawberries.
Tel: 63 09 40.

PUIGPUNYENT
The English Rose PP
Tiny English-run restaurant hiding in a mountain village.
Next to the church. Tel: 61 41 80. Closed Monday.

PORT DE SÓLLER
Es Canyis PP
Casual seafront restaurant with Mallorcan and French food.
Passeig Platja. Tel: 63 14 06.

SÓLLER
Sa Cova d'en Jordi PP
Neat, friendly restaurant in town centre serving Mallorcan and international fare.
Plaça Constitució 7. Tel: 63 32 22.
Closed Wednesday.

Celler Ca's Carrete P
Useful bar-restaurant by the main bus stop serving local food to locals.
Plaça America 5. Tel: 63 03 64.

VALLDEMOSSA
Hostal Ca'n Mario PP
On the first floor in an old-style *hostal*. Simple Mallorcan menu and beaming service.
Carrer de Uetam 8. Tel: 61 21 22. Closed Tuesday.
Ca'n Pedro PP
Opposite the main car park. Quiet and friendly when there are no tourist coaches, Mallorcan food.
Carrer de Arxiduc L Salvador 6.
Tel: 61 21 70. Closed Monday.

NORTHEAST
CALA D'OR
Bistro PP
Charcoal grills and international menu, for that special night out.
Carrer Andres Roig 7. Tel: 65 81 10.
Yate d'Or PP
Popular restaurant with patio, serving seafood and international dishes.
Avinguda Belgica 4. Tel: 65 79 78.

CAPDEPERA
Porxada de Sa Torre PP
Next to Torre de Canyamel, a spacious *rancho*-style barn with wooden tables. Mostly meat dishes.
Carretera de Canyamel–Artà km5.
Tel: 56 30 44.

PETRA
Moli d'en Pau PP
Country restaurant, partly in a renovated windmill, with good service and mostly Mallorcan food.
Carretera Santa Margalida km25.
Tel: 85 51 18.

Sa Creu P
Modern roadside stop on the Petra by-pass. Wholesome Mallorcan food fit for lorry drivers.
Carretera Manacor–Inca km9.
Tel: 83 02 46.

POLLENÇA
La Font del Gall PP
Small French-owned restaurant with good food, wine and – a rare find – proper desserts.
Carrer de Montesió. Tel: 53 03 96. Closed Monday.

PORT DE POLLENÇA
La Fortalesa PP
Well-established bar, restaurant and cafeteria with a good selection of *tapas* and local dishes.
Carretera Formentor. Tel: 53 10 59.
Los Faroles P
A pleasant, simple seafront restaurant which is very popular with the local inhabitants.
Passeig Saralegui 46. No telephone.
Stay PP
First class restaurant with extensive local and international menu and a terrace overlooking the harbour.
Muelle Nuevo. Tel: 53 00 13. Closed Monday.

PORTO PETRO
Ca'n Martina PP
Waterfront location offering fresh fish, paellas and delicious homemade cakes and tarts.
Passeig des Port. Tel: 65 75 17.

SA COLÒNIA DE SANT PERE
El Pescador PP
Fresh fish invariably caught from the owner's boat.
Carrer de Sant Joan 58. Tel: 58 90 78.

SON SERVERA
S'Era de Pula PPP
High class, old farmhouse-style dining with Mallorcan and fish specialities.
Carretera de Son Servera–Capdepera km3.
Tel: 56 79 40. Closed Monday.

SOUTH
ALGAIDA
Es 4 Vents PP
Well-known restaurant with a high standard of Mallorcan cooking.
Carretera de Palma–Manacor km21.
Tel: 66 51 73. Closed Thursday.

CAN PASTILLA
El Rancho Picadero PP
Roast meats with terrace and barbecue outside.
Carrer de Flamenco 1. Tel: 26 10 02.
Closed Monday.

FELANITX
Son Colom PP
Popular roadhouse useful when touring the southeast.
1km west of Felanitx on the road to Campos. Tel: 58 10 76.

SA COLÒNIA DE SANT JORDI
El Puerto PP
Fresh fish and paellas attract both locals and tourists.
Carrer de Port 13. Tel: 65 60 47.
Ses Roques PP
Large farmhouse with fish a speciality.
Carretera de Sa Colònia de Sant Jordi–Campos. Tel: 65 10 47.

SES COVETES
S'Escar PP
Beach bar-restaurant serving simple fish dishes and paellas.
Western end of Platja es Trenc.
Tel: 83 82 73.

Hotels and Accommodation

*T*he bulk of accommodation on Mallorca consists of hotels and apartment complexes catering for holidaymakers. As the island's tourist boom started back in the 1960s, some buildings are now out-dated – even abandoned. Today there is a more intelligent attitude to architectural style and the planning of resorts. Standards are rising, alternative forms of accommodation are on the increase and the days of predictable, repetitive hotels appear numbered.

RESORT HOTELS

Most visitors to the island have pre-paid accommodation as part of a package deal. This is by far the cheapest way of staying on Mallorca as the large operators have the economic muscle to get rooms at low prices. It is possible in the low season to take a flight and get bargain accommodation, or to negotiate favourable rates for a long stay – as some overwintering senior citizens do. Package holidays with accommodation allocated only on arrival are even more economical.

Spanish hotels are graded by stars from 1 to 5. Tour operators also have their own classifications based on different criteria, such as if balconies have a sea view (plenty do not). The difference between a 2- and 3-star hotel is not always great. Even though the holiday market is highly competitive, the adage that you get what you pay for generally holds true. Some hotels have particular specialities, such as extensive sports facilities, access to a golf course, or closeness to walking or birdwatching areas.

LUXURY ACCOMMODATION

The standard of accommodation and ambience in 4- and 5-star hotels is markedly different to that of lower grades. In particular, the choice and standard of entertainment laid on in the evenings can be very good.

Luxury hotels close to Palma include the **Arabella Golf**, **Son Vida** and **Valparaiso Palace**. In the north of the island, the **Hotel Formentor** on Cap de Formentor has been pampering the rich

Most rooms in resort hotels have balconies, but you may have to pay extra for a sea view

Arabella Golf Hotel, Son Vida: among the best on the island

and famous since 1926, while **La Residencia** in Deià attracts a well-off hip clientele. For those with the wherewithal, villas with swimming pool and domestic staff can be rented (see page 174). There are no Paradors (state-owned luxury hotels) in the Balearic Islands.

APARTMENTS
An apartment increases your holiday options – you can cook your own food or eat in your associated hotel or a nearby restaurant. Supermarkets are never far away, and many families prefer this less structured type of holiday. The Spanish authorities grade their *apartamentos turísticos* (AT) into four classes symbolised with keys. Apartment complexes can be found in all the resorts but are particularly common along the Calvià coast, and at Peguera, Cala Millor and Port d'Alcúdia.

RESERVATIONS
A comprehensive annual guide to accommodation on the island, *Hoteles,* *Campings, Apartementos,* is available from tourist offices. Hotel reservations can be made through the Central de Reservas de la Federación Empresarial Hotelera de Mallorca (tel: 20 84 59; fax: 75 65 46).

Six per cent IVA (value added tax) is added to hotel bills, 15 per cent in 5-star hotels. Unless you are on a package holiday, breakfast is not normally included in the price of a room.

COMPLAINTS
Not all the hotels in Mallorca are as good as the glossy brochures suggest. Problems like noise, building work, rooms with a view of the rubbish bins and low quality or damaged furnishings do arise. If you have cause for complaint, contact your tour representative who will regularly visit your hotel. In the event of a major grievance, or if you feel you have not received value for money, gather evidence that can back your case, perhaps by taking photographs. All hotels and restaurants have a complaints book where you can officially lodge a grievance.

Hotels and apartment complexes in Illetes. Some cliff-top hotels have lifts to the beach

VILLAS AND FARMHOUSES

Recent initiatives to widen the appeal of the island have led to an increase in the opportunities for a holiday amid the tranquillity and beauty of the Mallorcan countryside. A select band of country houses have now been turned into hotels, such as **L'Hermitage** in Orient, and a number of rural homes and working farms have been converted into appealing places to stay for a week or two. All quite individual, these are usually stone buildings decorated with rustic furniture and Spanish textiles. Facilities are of a high standard, with a garden, patio, swimming pool and open fire.

Villas and farmhouses in Mallorca can be booked through specialist operators. A *Vivre Mallorca* brochure with details of properties on the island is available from Spanish tourist offices. For reservations tel: 20 84 59.

BUDGET ACCOMMODATION

Last minute or off-season package holidays can provide a cheap and easy way to stay in Mallorca. There are no youth hostels or student-orientated dormitories on the island. For low-priced accommodation there are 1- and 2-star hotels, *hostales* (H) which are rated 1 to 3 stars, and *pensiónes* (P). These classifications, along with *fondas* (F) (inns) – and *Casas de Huéspedes* (CH) (guesthouses) are only of interest to bureaucrats and provide no easy guide to price, cleanliness or comfort. Palma offers the greatest selection of such accommodation, but most towns and ports have a *hostal* or two – though finding vacancies in the summer can be a problem. Always ask to see the room before you accept it.

HOSTERÍAS (RELIGIOUS HOSTELRIES)

Mallorca's many religious sanctuaries have a long tradition of hospitality, offering simple accommodation to passing visitors. Their remote locations will appeal to people happy to be away from the bright lights, but they are not intended as a source of a cheap holiday. If you are content to stay the night in premises solely concerned with the worship of God, most likely in the company of other pilgrims, places like the **Ermita de Sant Salvador** (near Felanitx, see page 121) and **Ermita de Nostra Senyora de Cura** (Puig de Randa, see page 125) continue to offer sanctuary to those who desire it.

Rooms are spartan with only a wash basin, and guests are expected to make up their bed and take breakfast communally. At the monastery of **Lluc** (see page 72) the atmosphere is slightly more relaxed, and during the summer religious students, pilgrim families from abroad and casual visitors all stay in its dormitory-style accommodation. Meals are available here and in other sanctuaries.

CAMPING

There are only two official campsites in Mallorca, both of which get crowded in summer, and the tourist authorities do not actively encourage visitors to bring caravans or motorhomes to their small island. As on the Spanish mainland, camping with a tent is only permitted outside sites if you have prior permission from the landowner.

Camping Platja Blava, Platja del Muro. 1st class. A large level site close to the sandy beach at Platja de Muro and within walking distance of the S'Albufera nature reserve. There are many static caravans and it can get noisy at peak season and weekends. Facilities include swimming pool, tennis courts, electric hook-up.
Tel: 53 78 63. Open: all year.
Club San Pedro, Sa Colònia de Sant Pere. 3rd class. A small park beside a narrow rock and pebble beach at the eastern end of this fishing port. There is a small pool, a bar-restaurant and electric hook-up.
Tel: 58 90 23. Open: April–September.

Take a balcony seat as the sun sets

On Business

*L*ess than a two-hour flight from many European cities, Mallorca is an island where business and leisure are easily combined. Having grown rich from welcoming guests from abroad, it presents few problems to the business man or woman dropping in for a few days. However, for longer term projects, such as starting a business or buying property, it is essential to seek professional help.

BANKS

Quotes for foreign exchange transactions are available by phone (*fonocambio*) from Banca March, tel: 46 28 19.

BUSINESS HOURS

Office hours are normally 9am–1.30pm and 4.30–7pm. Banks and shops are open on Saturday mornings.

BUSINESS SERVICES

Car Hire

Avis, Passeig Marítim 19, Palma. Tel: 73 07 20.
Hertz, Passeig Marítim 13, Palma. Tel: 73 47 37.
Serra Rent-a-Car, Carrer de Vaixell, Can Pastilla. Tel: 26 94 11.

Courier Services

DHL, Plaça del Progres 11, Palma. Tel: 45 53 53.

Office, Secretarial and Translation Services

Intelcom, Carrer de J Crespi 38, Palma. Tel: 45 83 87.
Network Business, Avinguda Joan Miró 149, Palma. Tel: 40 25 07.
Progreso Language School, Plaça del Progres, Palma. Tel: 71 46 13.

Travel Arrangements

July and August are very busy months on the island and accommodation or facilities may need to be booked well in advance.

Iberia Airlines, Passeig des Born 10, Palma. Tel: 71 80 00.
Trasmediterranea, Estacio Marítim 2, Muelle de Paraires, Palma.
Tel: 40 50 14.
Viajes Marsans, Carrer de Catalunya 4, Palma. Tel: 28 51 50.

CONFERENCE AND EXHIBITION FACILITIES

Palma has two principal conference venues.
Palacio de Congresos, Carrer de Poble Espanyol 39. Tel: 23 70 70.
Part of a best-of-Spain architectural theme park in the west of the city. See page 41.
Auditòrium, Passeig Marítim 18.
Tel: 23 53 28.
A 1,700-seater auditorium on the seafront with one of the largest stages in Spain, also used for cultural events.

For information on all aspects of conventions and conferences:
Mallorca Convention Bureau, Poble Espanyol, Carrer de Poble Espanyol 39.
Tel: 73 92 02.

Events organisers, including excursions, equipment and staff:
Kontiki, Passeig Marítim 13, Palma.
Tel: 28 48 08.

HOTELS

Most large hotels have a conference

room and *bureau de change*. Several have business floors, satellite TV, business centres and audiovisual equipment.

Travellers who buy tickets through Thomas Cook are entitled to use the services of a Thomas Cook Network location to make hotel reservations free of charge. In Palma this is Viajes Marsans (see **Travel Arrangements** opposite for address).

Hotels with business facilities include:
Arabella Golf, Carrer de la Vinagrella, Palma. Tel: 79 98 99.
Bon Sol, Passeig d'Illetes 30, Illetes. Tel: 40 21 11.
Meliá Victoria, Avinguda Joan Miró 21, Palma. Tel: 23 43 42.
Son Vida, Castell Son Vida, Palma. Tel: 79 00 00.
Valparaiso Palace, La Bonanova, Palma. Tel: 40 04 11.

LEISURE
Club Elite, Carrer de Joan Miró 334, Palma. Tel: 40 20 80.
Fitness centre, squash courts, sauna, restaurant.
Cruceros Iberia, Moll Vell 6G, Palma. Tel: 71 71 90.
Charter and excursion boats.

For golf facilities, see page 162.

SHOPS
Useful shops in the centre of Palma.
Body Shop, Plaça del Mercat 11. Tel 71 27 41.
C&A, Plaça Rei Carles I. Tel: 71 06 48.
Galeria Preciados, Avinguda de Jaume III, 15. Tel: 29 42 00.
Libreria Fondevilas (bookshop), Costa de la Pols 18. Tel: 72 56 17.

Spanish banks are normally closed by 2pm

Percay (luggage), Carrer de Constitució 5. Tel: 71 41 32.
Novolent (opticians), Avinguda Jaume III 25. Tel: 71 53 24.

TELEPHONE NUMBERS
The *Balears Guia Telefònica* (Balearic Islands Telephone Directory) has useful numbers in its introductory pages, including international dialling codes. Addresses are arranged by town.
Airport: 26 46 66.
Ajuntament (Town Hall): 72 77 44.
Ambulance: 20 41 11.
Iberia Airlines (Information): 26 26 00.
Police: 091.
Taxi (Palma) 40 14 14.
Tourist Office (Palma): 71 22 16
Weather: 094.

Practical Guide

ARRIVING
Documents
Citizens of European Union countries,
USA, Canada, New Zealand and Japan
who hold valid passports do not require
a visa to visit Spain for periods of less
than 90 days. Other travellers should
check with their nearest Spanish
Consulate.

By air
Iberia, the Spanish national airline,
operates scheduled flights to Palma
from destinations in Spain and Europe.
Viva Air, the leisure specialist of the
Iberia Group, operate scheduled flights
from London Heathrow to Palma.

The island is also served by many
other airlines and charter flights.

For Iberia call: (Palma) 71 80 00;
(Madrid) (91) 587 87 87; (London)
0171-830 0011.

Son Sant Joan airport is 11km east
of Palma and connected by motorway
to the capital. There are two terminals,
A for scheduled flights and B for
charter. A new terminal is under
construction with the first stages due for
completion by summer 1996. The
airport has a full range of facilities
including souvenir shops, car rental,
post office and hotel booking services.
There is a tourist information counter
in the Terminal B Arrivals lounge.

Bus 17 runs from the airport to the
centre of Palma, or you can take a taxi.

On departure, there is a large duty-
free shop which you can visit after
passing passport and security controls.
If you are travelling at peak times on
charter flights, make sure you have
some *pesetas* and entertainment on hand
in case of delay ('*Retrasado* ' on the
flight information screen); '*Embarcando*'
means 'Boarding'.
Airport Information, tel: 26 46 24.
Iberia Airlines Information,
tel: 26 26 00.
Tourist Information, tel: 26 08 03.

Iberia, Spain's national airline

By sea

Trasmediterránea operate daily connections by car and passenger ferry from Barcelona and Valencia to Palma. Reservations can be made at travel agents or Estació Marítimo no 2, Palma (tel: 40 50 14). They also sail between Palma and Mahón (Menorca) and Ibiza. For further information:
Barcelona, tel: (3) 412 25 24.
Valencia, tel: (6) 367 65 12.
Mahón, tel: 36 29 50.
Ibiza, tel: 31 41 73.

    Flebasa Lines operate a regular car and passenger hydrofoil/ferry service from Dénia (Alicante) to Palma via Ibiza, and between Port d'Alcúdia and Ciutadella (Menorca).
General enquiries, tel: 31 40 05.
Palma, tel: 40 53 60.
Port d'Alcúdia, tel: 54 64 54.

CAMPING, see page 175.

CHILDREN

Nappies, baby food and formula milk can be bought in Mallorca but if you have a preferred brand of quality take it with you. Not all hotels and restaurants have sufficient high chairs, so if you have your own screw-on type take it. If you need to hire a car seat for a child, double check availability when making the booking. See also pages 158–9.

CLIMATE

Most people visit Mallorca between April and September when the island is invariably warm and sunny. July and August are the hottest and driest months. Rain is most likely between October and February, when it can be quite cold.

WEATHER CONVERSION CHART
25.4mm = 1 inch
°F = 1.8 × °C + 32

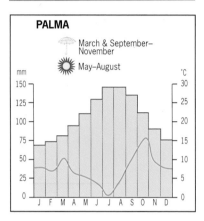

PALMA

March & September–November

May–August

CONSULATES
UK: Plaça Major 3D, Palma.
Tel: 71 24 45.
USA: Avinguda Jaume III 26, Palma.
Tel: 72 26 60.

CONVERSION TABLES
See opposite.

CRIME
According to Robert Graves, Mallorca was once 'the most crime-free island in Europe'. Times have, alas, changed and commonsense precautions against petty crime are essential. Beware of pickpockets in markets, outside tourist sights and in crowded places. If you are harassed by what the tour reps call 'colourful characters' trying to sell carnations, tablecloths or watches keep moving and never get any money out as it will only exacerbate the problem.

Thefts can be carried out by your fellow holidaymakers too – apartments

Conversion Table

FROM	TO	MULTIPLY BY
Inches	Centimetres	2.54
Feet	Metres	0.3048
Yards	Metres	0.9144
Miles	Kilometres	1.6090
Acres	Hectares	0.4047
Gallons	Litres	4.5460
Ounces	Grams	28.35
Pounds	Grams	453.6
Pounds	Kilograms	0.4536
Tons	Tonnes	1.0160

To convert back, for example from centimetres to inches, divide by the number in the the third column.

Men's Suits

UK		36	38	40	42	44	46	48
Rest of Europe	46	48	50	52	54	56	58
US		36	38	40	42	44	46	48

Dress Sizes

UK		8	10	12	14	16	18
France	36	38	40	42	44	46
Italy	38	40	42	44	46	48
Rest of Europe	34	36	38	40	42	44
US		6	8	10	12	14	16

Men's Shirts

UK	14	14.5	15	15.5	16	16.5	17
Rest of Europe	36	37	38	39/40	41	42	43
US	14	14.5	15	15.5	16	16.5	17

Men's Shoes

UK	7	7.5	8.5	9.5	10.5	11
Rest of Europe	41	42	43	44	45	46
US	8	8.5	9.5	10.5	11.5	12

Women's Shoes

UK	4.5	5	5.5	6	6.5	7
Rest of Europe	38	38	39	39	40	41
US	6	6.5	7	7.5	8	8.5

are particularly vulnerable in this respect. Never carry large amounts of cash or valuables, and always use safe deposit boxes in hotels – the small fee is worth it. Leave nothing you care about in your car or unattended on a beach. If you are unhappy about carrying your passport, get a photocopy of it verified and stamped at a police station.

CUSTOMS REGULATIONS

Spain is part of the European Union, so there are no restrictions on the movement of duty-paid goods for personal use between Mallorca and other EU countries. If you make purchases in EU duty-free shops such as at the airport, or aboard planes and ships, then certain maximum allowances come into force. The current limits are well advertised.

DISABLED TRAVELLERS

Several package holiday operators cater for disabled visitors to Mallorca and can provide information on the facilities available at the hotels they use. Access to many sights remains a problem, but a benign climate, long level seafronts and the proximity of qualified medical attention are all positive reasons for visiting Mallorca.

Local facilities for the disabled (*minusváslido*) include:
EMT Bus Special Service,
tel: 29 57 00.
Taxi 604 Minusválido, tel: 40 14 14.
Federación de Deportes de Minusválidos, tel: 27 16 90.

DRESS

The Spanish believe beachwear and swimming costumes belong at the seaside. You may be refused entry to Palma cathedral and other churches, as

If in doubt, ask a Mallorcan policeman

well as some banks, shops and restaurants, if you are considered to be improperly dressed. Topless sunbathing is common on many beaches, but nudism is confined to more remote beaches.

DRIVING

A car is not essential to enjoy Mallorca, but it is the best way to see the island at your own pace.

Car rental

Mallorca is overrun with car rental companies. If you intend to collect a car at the airport, or need a child seat, make arrangements before you leave home. Drivers normally have to be over 21 and to have held a licence for at least six months.

It is advisable to take out comprehensive insurance and Collision Damage Waiver. Twelve per cent IVA (VAT) is added to bills.

On the road

Drive on the right. Speed limits are 120kph on motorways, 100kph on main roads, 90kph on other roads except in urban areas, where it is 60kph or as signposted. Seat belts are compulsory in front seats. Vigilance is required, particularly on mountain roads. If you meet a coach, you are obliged to reverse.

Palma is usefully by-passed by a ringroad known as Via Cintura. An *autopista* (motorway) runs west to Peguera, and another northeast almost as far as Inca. A third extends south past the airport to S'Arenal.

Parking

Parking restrictions are enforced by a scheme known as ORA. In town centres, parking lots marked in blue with Zona Blava (Blue Zone) signs can only be used with a ticket bought in advance from a newsagent's or tobacconist's. These are valid for 30–90 minutes and have to be marked and displayed before you leave the car. Failure to do this can result in fines, wheel-clamping or your vehicle being towed away.

In Palma ORA is in force within the boundaries of the old city walls between Monday and Friday 9.30am–1.30pm and 5–8pm. If you need to stay longer, go to a public car park. In Palma there are car parks on the seafront and beneath Plaça Major. If the weather is hot, a sun-shield under the windscreen is advisable. Leave no valuables behind.

Petrol

Petrol is *gasolina* and unleaded *sin plomo*. Petrol stations are normally open 6am–10pm, closed Sundays and holidays. Addresses of 24-hour petrol stations are printed in the *Majorca Daily Bulletin*. Larger garages are self-service and normally take credit cards.

ELECTRICITY

220–225 volts. Sockets take round two-pin style plugs, so an adaptor may be required.

EMERGENCY TELEPHONE NUMBERS

In any emergency dial 091.
Fire Brigade: Bomberos, 080.
Medical Help: Cruz Roja, 29 50 00.
Casa de Socorro Palma, 72 21 79.
Casa de Socorro Alcúdia, 54 63 71.

For Thomas Cook travellers' cheque refund, ring 900 99 4403 (toll free, 24-hour service). Loss or theft should be reported within 24 hours.

MasterCard holders can use any Thomas Cook Network location to report the loss or theft of their card, and to obtain an emergency replacement. This is a free service under the Thomas Cook MasterCard Alliance. In Mallorca contact Viajes Marsans, Carrer de Catalunya 4, Palma. Tel: 28 51 50.

HEALTH

There are no mandatory vaccination requirements for entering Mallorca, but tetanus and polio immunisation should be kept up to date. As in many parts of the world, AIDS is present. Take a strong suntan cream, anti-diarrhoea pills and, particularly if you are staying in the Badia d'Alcúdia area, mosquito repellent. If you need to consult a doctor (*médico*) or dentist (*dentista*), ask at your hotel reception. **Clinic Balear** (tel: 46 62 62) offer 24-hour medical services from centres around the island.

When you arrive in your hotel or apartment spend a few minutes checking that balcony railings are secure, there is an unobstructed fire exit, cots and children's equipment are safe, and that you cannot lock yourself out by the balcony door. Report any smell of gas, check swimming pools for concealed walls before diving in, and avoid food that appears undercooked or reheated.

EU citizens are entitled to reciprocal

medical benefits in Spain and should obtain the relevant document before travelling. Not all doctors offer treatment under this scheme, and you need first to contact the Instituto National de la Seguridad Social (INSS) to obtain treatment vouchers. The central office in Palma is at La Rambla 18 (tel: 72 31 00).

Insurance

Adequate medical insurance is highly recommended – and is a pre-travel requirement with many package holidays. In the UK this can be purchased through the AA, branches of Thomas Cook and most travel agents.

Travellers who purchase travel tickets through Thomas Cook are entitled to free emergency assistance at any Thomas Cook Network location as part of the Thomas Cook Worldwide Customer Promise. In Mallorca this is Viajes Marsan (see **Emergency Telephone Numbers**).

LOST PROPERTY

If you lose anything of value inform the police, if only for insurance purposes. The loss of a passport should be reported to your consulate. In theory objects that are found and handed in make their way to the local Ajuntament (town hall). In Palma this is at Plaça Cort 1 (tel: 72 77 44 ext. 1165).

LANGUAGE

The following words may solve a few mysteries.

English	Catalan	Castilian
Sunday	diumenge	domingo
Monday	dilluns	lunes
Tuesday	dimarts	martes
Wednesday	dimerces	miércoles
Thursday	dijous	jueves
Friday	divendres	viernes
Saturday	dissabte	sábado
open	obert	abierto
closed	tancat	cerrado
holiday	festa	festivo
beach	platja	playa
street	carrer	calle
avenue	avinguda	avenida
quay	moll	muelle
bay	badia	bahía
church	església	iglesia
ticket	bitllet	billete
today	avui	hoy
tomorrow	demà	mañana
please	si us plau	por favor
thank you	gràcies	gracias

Forn des Teatre, Palma – the Theatre Bakery

MAPS

A more up-to-date map than most is the red-covered *Mallorca* from TD (Distrimapas Telstar), on sale in some newsagents.

MEDIA

Foreign newspapers and magazines can be bought from newsagents in the centre of Palma and in the larger resorts. The English-language *Majorca Daily Bulletin*, includes useful local information and comment as well as topical stories. The bi-monthly *Mallorca Tourist Info* is printed in English, German, Dutch and Swedish and contains reports and advertisements about things to do on the island. *The Reader* is an English-language weekly newspaper covering all the Balearics, while the glossy weekly lifestyle magazine *Balearic Leisure and Living* is published in Spanish and English.

The local newspapers are *Diario de Mallorca*, *Última Hora*, *Baleares* and *El Día 16*. In the Balearic Islands there are television channels broadcasting in both Catalan and Castilian. Satellite channels are received in some hotels and bars in the large resorts.

MONEY MATTERS

The Spanish unit of currency is the peseta. Banknotes are issued for 1,000, 2,000, 5,000 and 10,000 pesetas; coins for 1, 5, 10, 25, 50, 100, 200 and 500 pesetas. Credit cards can be widely used in Palma and the resorts, but take cash as a back-up if you are going to shops or restaurants off the tourist track.

Thomas Cook Mastercard travellers' cheques avoid the hazards of carrying large amounts of cash, and can be quickly refunded in the event of their loss or theft. Peseta cheques are recommended, but cheques in US dollars and some other European currencies are accepted. Many hotels, large restaurants and some shops will accept travellers' cheques in lieu of cash. You will need your passport when using them.

OPENING TIMES

Banks: Monday to Friday 9am–2pm, Saturday 9am–1pm.

Churches: often 8am–1pm and 5–8pm, but there is no set pattern. On Sunday churches are open as services permit (sightseeing is not welcomed while acts of worship are in progress).

Museums: at least 10am–1pm and 4–6pm, often longer. Opening hours are reduced in the winter, and most close for for at least one day a week.

Shops: Monday to Friday 9.30 or 10am until 1 or 2pm, then around 4.30–8pm or even later in summer. On Saturday shops open in the morning only. See page 142.

PHARMACIES

Chemists (*farmacias*) in Spain are obvious from the green cross outside. Unlike *droguerías*, which sell toiletries and perfume, they are devoted to dispensing medication and can be useful sources of advice and treatment for minor ailments. Addresses and opening times of duty chemists open outside normal hours are posted in pharmacy windows and printed in local papers, including the *Majorca Daily Bulletin*.

PLACES OF WORSHIP

Mallorca is Roman Catholic. Visitors are free to attend Mass in local churches, some of which hold services in English. A comprehensive list of places of worship catering for different faiths and nationalities is available from tourist offices. The larger hotels can often supply details of local services.

Anglican Church, Carrer de Nunyez de Balboa 6, Palma. Tel: 73 72 79. Services on Sunday and Wednesday.

Catholic Church of San Fernando, Carretera S'Arenal 308, Las Maravillas. Tel: 26 28 93. Daily service in German, plus English and French on Sunday.

High Mass in Palma Cathedral on Sunday is at 10.30am.

POLICE

There are three types. The urban-based Policía Municipal wear blue and have the thankless task of keeping the traffic under control. The Policía Nacional wear brown and uphold law and order in towns and cities. The Guardia Civil wear green and control the highways and country areas. Some resorts have their own tourist-friendly police, the Policía Turística. If you need a police station, ask for *la comisaría*.

Policía Municipal, Carrer de Sant

Post your letter then catch the bus

Ferran, Palma. Tel: 28 06 06.

Policía Nacional, Carrer de Ruiz Alda 8, Palma. Tel: 28 04 00.

Guardia Civil, Carrer de Manuel Azana 10, Palma. Tel: 46 51 12.

POST OFFICES

The main post office (*correus*) in Palma is just east of Passeig des Born at Carrer de Constitució 5 (tel: 72 10 95). It is open Monday to Friday 9am–9pm, Saturday 9am–2pm. Other post offices are generally open Monday to Friday 9am–1pm and 4–7pm, morning only on Saturday. Letters can be sent to a post office for collection (marked Lista de Correos) – take your passport when you collect them.

Stamps (*sellos*) can also be bought from tobacconists – look for a brown and yellow sign saying 'Tabacos'. Many hotels stock them, as do most smart-thinking shops that sell postcards. Letter-boxes are yellow.

PUBLIC HOLIDAYS

1 January New Year's Day
6 January Epiphany
Variable Good Friday and Easter Monday
1 May Labour Day
Variable (May/June) Corpus Christi
15 August Assumption
12 October Discovery of America
1 November All Saints' Day
8 December Immaculate Conception
25 and 26 December Christmas

These are holidays throughout Spain. For additional local holidays and festivities see pages 156–7.

PUBLIC TRANSPORT

Bus

The bus system in Mallorca is good. Services are cheap and efficient and the timetables posted at *paradas* (bus stops), and available free from tourist offices, are generally reliable. Pay as you enter and keep hold of your ticket as inspectors frequently board the buses. The island's central bus station is in Plaça d'Espanya in Palma, where there is an information kiosk and tourist office. In the city buses are run by EMT; useful routes include:

1 Passeig Marítim–Plaça d'Espanya
15 S'Arenal – Can Pastilla–Plaça d'Espanya
17 Aeroport–Plaça d'Espanya
21 Palma Nova–Plaça de la Reina–Plaça d'Espanya.

For EMT (Palma) bus information, tel: 29 08 55.

Horse-drawn carriage

Sundays, when there is less traffic, is the best time to ride round the historic centre of Palma by horse and carriage. There are ranks of *galeras* along Passeig de Sagrera and beside the cathedral in Costa de la Seu. A sign displays tariffs, and a tip is expected.

Go sightseeing in Palma by horse and carriage

Taxi

Taxis are black and white and can be hailed in the street or picked up at ranks in Palma and major towns and resorts. A green light and sign saying 'Lliure/Libre' indicates they are available for hire. Prices are reasonable but increase at night and weekends. If you are travelling a long distance, negotiate the fare first. To call a taxi:
Radio Taxi, tel: 75 54 40
Palma, tel: 40 14 14.

Train

Mallorca has two narrow-gauge railway lines. Trains depart from adjacent stations in Plaça d'Espanya, one route running north to Sóller (55 minutes) and the other – with a more frequent service – travelling east to Inca (35 minutes). For information:
Palma–Sóller, tel: 75 20 51
Palma–Inca, tel: 75 22 45.

There are plenty of trains between Palma and Inca, promoted as the 'Leather Express'

Tram

A historic tram line runs between Sóller and Port de Sóller (30 minutes). See page 83.

SENIOR CITIZENS

Mallorca attracts a good number of senior citizens, particularly in the low and 'shoulder' seasons when life is more relaxed and prices more reasonable. Some tour operators offer special extended stay deals if you want to escape to Mallorca for the winter. It is advisable to take out full medical and travel insurance prior to your departure.

TELEPHONES

The Spanish telephone system is good and, with the increasing availability of Credifone kiosks that accept phonecards, there is little need to pay the high costs of international calls from a hotel bedroom. Phonecards (Credifone) can be bought from post offices and *Tabacos* for a minimum of 500 pesetas.

Payphones

A public telephone (*teléfono*) takes a variety of coins, 25 pesetas will be enough for a local call – garner a pile of 100-peseta coins if you are calling abroad. The coins should be lined up in the slot before you dial. Rates are cheaper between 10pm and 8am. Many bars have a payphone.

You can also make calls from the Locutori Public Telefónica booths in resorts – you pay a cashier after making the call, which is metered. In Palma there is a Telefónica opposite the main post office, at Carrer de Constitució 1. It is open 9am–8pm and includes a fax service.

Coffee with the stars in Plaça del Mercat, Palma. It may cost more to sit outside

Dialling Codes

If you are calling the Balearic Islands from outside Spain the code is 71, within Spain 971. To make an international call from Mallorca dial 07 then the country code. Some international codes are: Australia 61, Canada and USA 1, Irish Republic 353, New Zealand 64, UK 44.

Useful numbers
Operator: 002
Directory Enquiries (Mallorca): 78 03 03
Directory Enquiries (Spain): 003
Weather: 094
International Directory Enquiries: 025.

TIME

The time in the Balearic Islands is the same as that on mainland Spain. Spain is one hour ahead of Greenwich Mean Time (GMT). Spanish Summer Time, when the clocks are put forward an hour, is from the last Sunday of March to the last Sunday of September.

TIPPING

Tipping is the norm in Spain. In restaurants a service charge is usually included in the price, but people often leave tips as well. Leave a few coins for bar staff or waiters, give a few hundred pesetas to porters, maids, coach drivers and guides, consider 10 per cent for meals and taxis.

TOILETS

Public toilets are not common in Mallorca, and if you find them they are unlikely to have paper. As the tour guides like to put it, go while the going is good. You do not have to be a customer to use the services of a bar or restaurant, but it is polite to ask first.

Toilets are variously described as *servicios* and *aseos* and heralded by entertaining pictograms intended to crystallise the difference between the sexes: *señores*, *hombres* and *caballeros* are for pipe-smoking dudes while ladies with dark curls and dangerous-looking earrings should go for *señoras* and *damas*. Facilities are generally modern, but don't bank on it.

TOURIST INFORMATION

For information on Mallorca before you leave home, there are Spanish National Tourist Offices in many cities around the world.

Overseas

Canada: Tourist Office of Spain, 14th floor, 102 Bloor St West, Toronto, Ontario M5S 1M8. Tel: (1416) 961 31 31.
UK: Spanish Tourist Office, 57 St James's St, London SW1A 1LD. Tel: 0171-499 0901.
USA: Tourist Office of Spain, 665 Fifth Avenue, New York, NY 10022. Tel: (1212) 759 88 22.

Spain

Barcelona: Gran Via de les Corts Catalanes 658. Tel: (93) 301 74 43.
Madrid: Edificio Torre de Madrid, Calle Princesa 1. Tel: (91) 541 23 25.

Mallorca

Information is available from tourist offices in Palma (see page 32) and in the following towns and resorts (see individual entries for addresses).
West of Palma: Cala Major (Illetes), Palma Nova (Magaluf), Peguera, Santa Ponça.
Northwest: Sóller, Port de Sóller, Valldemossa.
Northeast: Cala Millor, Cala Rajada, Can Picafort, Port d'Alcúdia, Port de Pollença.
South: Cala d'Or, Cala Figuera, Porto Cristo, Sa Colònia de Sant Jordi.
In summer offices are generally open Monday to Friday 9am–8pm and Saturday 9am–1.30pm. Small offices may be open shorter hours.

Flags outside the Consulat del Mar on Palma's seafront

ACKNOWLEDGEMENTS

The Automobile Association wishes to thank the following photographers and libraries for their assistance in the preparation of this book.

ARABELLA GOLF HOTEL 173
MARY EVANS PICTURE LIBRARY 70
IBERIA AIRLINES 179
INSTITUTO BALEAR DE PROMOCIAN DEL TURISMO 152, 154, 155, 157
INTERNATIONAL PHOTOBANK inset, 16b, 17a, 22, 23a,
NATURE PHOTOGRAPHERS LTD 111, 132b, 132c, 140a, 140b
H RAMSEY 136
SPECTRUM COLOUR LIBRARY cover, spine, 119a
H TISDALL 1, 54c, 63.

The remaining photographs are held in the Automobile Association's own library (AA PHOTO LIBRARY) and were taken by Peter Baker with the exception of pages 6, 17d, 19, 20, 24, 25b, 48, 54a, 55a, 55b, 58, 59, 61, 78/9, 80, 82, 87, 97a, 132a, 133, 139, 141, 143b, 161, 167, 175, 177 which were taken by Wyn Voysey.

The author would like to thank the following organisations and individuals for their assistance:
The staff of IBATUR, Fomento del Turismo de Mallorca and OIT Municipal de Palma. The Spanish Tourist Office in London, Affinity PIPR and TPS. Iberia Airlines, Thomson, Castaways, Royaltur and Serra Rent-a-Car. Mossèn Antoni M. Alcover and David Huelin for their book *Folk Tales of Mallorca* (Editorial Moll, Palma).

CONTRIBUTORS

Series adviser: Melissa Shales   **Designer:** Design 23   **Copy editor:** Audrey Horne
Verifier: Jenny Fry   **Indexer:** Marie Lorimer